Lee and Sarah's Girl

A Woman Scorned

by Violetta Elrod

Copyright © 2020 by Violetta Elrod

All rights reserved.

ISBN 978-1-62806-288-5 (print | paperback)
ISBN 978-1-62806-289-2 (print | hardback)

Library of Congress Control Number 2020914979

Published by Salt Water Media
29 Broad Street, Suite 104
Berlin, MD 21811
www.saltwatermedia.com

Cover images provided by author and author's family; cover and interior quilt artwork by Andrea Robinson-Berg

Violetta and Virginia circa 1963

Dedicated to my mother who began life on February 14th, 1911 as youngest daughter of Lee Bahnum Ruark and Sarah Martha Ruark. Depending on the documents and who's telling the story, Virginia was originally named Emma Jane or Imogene Ruark. Her various family members would refer to her in different ways depending on her mood and the circumstances. She was tenacious, persistent, and determined. She believed anything was possible. The impossible just might take a little longer. Her brother, Fred, once remarked, "She changed her name, residence and husband like some people change underwear." Sometimes it was Imogene/Emma Jane/Lady Jane/Lady Janey or Janey. In her mind, a new adventure demanded a new name so she was Jean/Jeanie/Missa Jeanie to her roomers and husband Paul Neumann in the 1940s. Later in life she became Virginia Lee/Virginia/Jinny to Maurice Cantwell. She was not easy to live with, but I truly loved her and always called her Mom.

*Front (left to right): Edna, Afrey, Fred, and Lee Bahnum
Back (left to right): Sarah Martha and Emma
circa 1913*

Author's Note:

On the opposite page is the earliest picture I have of the Ruark family. It was taken around 1913. My mother is about three years old and is the youngest in this photograph. She is sitting between her father, Lee Bahnum Ruark, and her mother, Sarah Martha Ruark. Her sister Edna and brothers, Afrey and Fred, are in the foreground. The older siblings had left home at the time this picture was taken. The first Ruark book entitled, *My Family Quilt*, tells the story of my family during the late 1800s and mid-1900s.

There were so many more stories to share I had to continue with my Mom's adventures, failures, and successes in this second book, *A Woman Scorned*. The cover photograph is of my Mom after she moved us to Wilmington in 1935 when I was just three years old.

These stories are set in the 1930s and 1940s. I experienced some of them firsthand. Some are family legend. The included maps and photographs are to help the reader get a sense of the people and places during that time. Many of those people and places are gone or changed beyond recognition. Some are still there but you must look closely to recognize them.

Cast Of Ruark Family Characters

Lee Bahnum Ruark married Sarah Martha and was Lee to Sarah, Pa to Virginia and PaPa to Violetta

Sarah Martha Ruark married Lee Ruark and was Saree to Lee, Ma to Virginia and MaMa to Violetta

Johnny Ruark married Frances and they were Uncle Johnny and Aunt Frances to Violetta

Roy Ruark married Grace and they were Uncle Roy and Aunt Grace to Violetta

Geneva, Doris Lee & Aleen Ruark Violetta's cousins and their parents were Roy and Grace Ruark

Carey Ruark Mumford married Tom Mumford and they were Aunt Carey and Uncle Tom to Violetta

Edna Ruark married Robert Pottle, Wayne Cloud and finally Weldon Parsons. She was Violetta's Aunt Edna

Bobby Pottle Jr. married Pansy and Aunt Edna was his mother

Shirley was Violetta's Cousin and Bobby and Pansy were her parents

Nina Pottle whose mother was Aunt Edna. She was called Aunt Nina by Violetta.

Joanne was Violetta's cousin and Aunt Nina was her mother

Norman Pottle was Violetta's cousin and Aunt Edna was his mother

Afrey Ruark died as a child before Violetta was born

Frederick Ruark married Katherin and was Uncle Fred and Aunt Katherin to Violetta

Nancy was Violetta's cousin and Uncle Fred and Aunt Katherin were her parents

Virginia Ruark married Ralph Corbin and eventually Paul Leopold Neumann

Paul Neumann was affectionately known as Dad to Violetta

Chapter 1 — A Woman Scorned

"Hell hath no fury like a woman scorned!" Janey's mother always said. She also said she really hated to say, "I told you so!" But she told Janey, her youngest daughter, every chance she got, "I told you so! Your husband, Ralph Corbin, couldn't keep a job in a pie shop. He's a grown man and he's too old to be playing with racing cars. He ought to get a job like those drummer salesmen who come down from Baltimore to sell us a lot of stuff we don't really need. With his glib tongue he'd be a great traveling salesman. I'll bet he could even sell ice to an Eskimo."

At first Janey defended her husband by saying there wasn't any future for him in selling anything. He had convinced her he was going to be a famous race car driver. He believed he would make a name for himself and get rich by racing. She was caught up in all the excitement at first. But after following him to so many of the races she grew tired of the whole thing. She gave him a big lecture on the fact they were parents now and he had a big responsibility. "Our baby girl is two years old and we are still dirt poor!" His answer, as usual, was, "I'm doing everything I can to become a famous race car driver. Then I'll make big money and be able to provide the best for you and our precious baby, Violetta!" He continued saying he didn't have time to argue with her about it today because he needed a new part for his car for the race next week in Ocean City. He dashed out the door with a hasty, "See you later." His buddies were going to drive him to Seaford, Delaware where someone said they had just the car part he needed to win this next race.

Janey had confided in Edna, her sister, how Ralph spent every spare minute and every spare cent he had on his car in his garage. He always told her the next race would be their ticket out of Salisbury. He won a few little races but there really wasn't much money to show for his efforts. It seemed like any money he won always had to go right back into making his car faster and easier to handle. He was a very good mechanic and was always able to think of ways to improve his car. This of course always called for another part he had to buy. Whenever he heard about a race in a different town, he would call his boss and pretend he was too sick to go to work. Then he would take off and sometimes be gone for days. His friends all tried to convince Janey he was a faithful husband and would never consider going out with another woman. She knew he wasn't fooling around with anyone because his car took all his spare time and all his spare cash. She often thought, *"I could deal with another woman who was messing with my man. But how can I fight with a car?"*

Today was their third wedding anniversary. The first mistake Ralph made, was just like a man, he forgot all about it! That was an unforgivable sin for Janey! Ralph was in such a hurry to leave and get to Seaford with his buddies he even forgot to lock his garage door. This was his second mistake. Janey's genetic makeup included very little patience. Add to that a whole lot of frustration. Match that with his neglect and her temper and you'd get something like an Eastern Shore hurricane brewing. Unfortunately, Ralph had made a third big mistake. He was in such a hurry to get his new car part he forgot to put his tools away. He left a large heavy crowbar sitting on the running board of his racing beauty. Janey completely lost control after he drove away with his friends.

She grabbed his crowbar and used it to demolish his car as well as her marriage. She broke everything breakable and smashed everything smashable. Then she opened the hood and continued her mayhem. The battery and the radiator were put out of commission permanently by jabbing them with his heavy crowbar. Every wire was torn out. The tires were slashed and went flatter than a pancake. Next, she broke out all the lights, the windshield, the back window, and all the side windows. Her final vicious acts were to rip all the upholstery and tear the side view mirrors off their brackets. She had run out of steam and stopped to catch her breath. Realizing now what she had done she sat down on the running board of Ralph's demolished car and cried until the sun had set.

Janey packed her suitcase and telephoned her sister, Edna, to come and get her and her baby, me, as soon as possible! Sarah, Edna's and Janey's mom, could be heard shouting in the background, "This here is family business! I'm coming too! Start your car, Edna, and wait till I get my hat."

Chapter 2 — Tough Decision

As Aunt Edna drove to her sister's house, she became lost in thoughts over some of the past events in her own life. She thought to herself, *"If I had the time, I think I could write a book about my life. It certainly hasn't been boring!"* She continued to think back over some of her memories.

"The first thing I remember was long ago when Robert Pottle bought my basket at our church social. A few days later he got permission from my father to call on me and begin his serious courting on Saturday at two o'clock.

She continued to think, *"I'll never forget what happened! It was Saturday afternoon and already two o'clock! I had been dressed for at least an hour. I was very nervous and excited. Robert and I were going to take our first buggy ride together without a chaperone. I worried maybe he'd changed his mind! I waited upstairs so he wouldn't get the idea I was too eager. But I really was! I heard a knock on the front door and mother called up the stairs, "Edna, Robert is here! Come on down!" Hoping to impress him I called downstairs and said, "Oh, I can't make up my mind, Ma. Which dress should I wear?" Much to my embarrassment she answered very loud and clear, "The same old brown one, Edna! The only one you've got! It's funny to remember now. But it wasn't funny then!"*

After our wedding I became Mrs. Pottle. Over time I had three children to raise Robert Junior, Nina, and little Norman. I never shared anything about my husband with anyone in the family. After my youngest son, Norman, was born Mr. Pottle just disappeared from the scene.

To be honest I thought, "Good riddance!" The only change I made was to stop referring to my oldest son as Robert and I started calling him Bobby. Maybe his father had died or went to *prison, or maybe he just walked away. I can't remember much about him now and I'm not about to dredge up the past. No one ever mentioned him, so it wasn't necessary for me to try and find out anything about him."*

Chapter 3 — Temper Tantrums

Edna continued to think as she drove to rescue her little sister. *"Norman, my youngest son, was a lot like my baby brother, Fred. He was always up to some little mischief or trick he enjoyed."* This thought from the past reminded her of one of Norman's many tricks and brought a broad smile to her face. *"When Norman was about three years old he had learned if he wanted something and couldn't get it he would let out a scream and cry. If he still didn't get what he wanted he'd fall to the floor and kick his feet furiously. If his screaming and kicking didn't work, he'd stop and hold his breath. He'd hold it so long he'd pass right out. Then I'd begin to panic and cry too. I loved him so much and I still do! I would always hold him gently, pat on him, and put whatever he wanted in his little hands. He often used this trick whenever another child had something he wanted. When he had one of those severe temper tantrums, I always gave his playmates one of my hard looks and they knew they'd better give in to him. If they didn't, they'd get a real hard smack from me!"*

(There were all kinds of discipline in those days before Doctor Spock came on the scene.)

Edna's thoughts were still racing through her mind. *This behavior worked for Norman until he was about five years old. Then he tried this trick on me again and I was just bone-tired on this day. My patience was worn thin and to the breaking point. I really didn't feel up to dealing rationally with his temper which he had got from me in the first place. When he passed out this time, I grabbed him up and ran out the door. It was so quiet you could have heard a mouse sneeze. Everyone watching did not know what to think. Was I going to try to run to the doctor's office or had I killed him? They were totally surprised to see me stop and lay him down on the pump bench. I then pumped the water up fast and furious. It splashed across his face and gushed into his mouth. All the neighbors and family watching were afraid I was going to drown him. He jumped up making choking sounds and was coughing a lot. Then I just walked back calmly into the kitchen and began to set the table for dinner. Everyone thought it was strange Norman has never ever had another temper tantrum. No one who saw my behavior ever said a word to me about this. But he never tried his little trick again and I could hear my PaPa, Lee Bahnum Ruark, saying, "There's more than one way to skin a cat!"*

*Janey and Norman (Edna's son)
circa 1929*

Chapter 4 — Don't Ask

Edna chuckled quietly and continued to think to herself. *"My son, Bobby and his wife, Pansy, were trying to find jobs to put food on the table and they had no one else to turn to for help. They asked if I would take care of their little girl, Shirley. My answer was, "Of course! Ain't I her MaMa?" But silently I thought, "More chickens have come home to roost." The family always said I was impatient and hard to live with. They said I had used up all my patience with my little brother, Afrey. I wasn't impatient or hard to live with. Everyone got along fine with me if they just did exactly what I said!"*

Edna strayed into thinking about how her grand-daughter, Shirley, had one time embarrassed her so badly. *"Brother Joseph, my mother's preacher, always came for a visit once a week. I thought he was just trying to get me to come to church with my mother. Today was the day for him to come for his weekly visit. I had made sure Shirley was clean and presentable. Then I told her to sit in the living room and wait for our visitor. I wanted to make a good impression, so I started straightening magazines on my end tables. About five minutes later I realized Shirley was not sitting where she was told. I was irritated now and yelled loudly for her, "Young lady, you better answer me and get in this house this minute!" I heard Shirley's little voice, "I'll be there in a minute. I'm busy!" "When Brother Joseph arrived, he and I talked for a few minutes. "By the way," he asked, "Where is your darling little granddaughter, Shirley? I heard she was staying with you. She is such a sweet child."*

"I answered Brother Joseph, "Oh, she's just outside playing." Trying not to show my agitation, I went to the back door and called out pleasantly, "Shirley, I want you to come inside now dear! What are you doing?" Shirley's little four-year-old sing-song voice came

loud and clear from the back yard, "I'm out here in the outhouse MaMa and I am shitting!"

Needless to say, Brother Joseph and I were both shocked and embarrassed. He pretended he had not heard Shirley. He glanced at his pocket watch and said, "Oh my, it's past time for my next house call! I really must be going now!"

(He didn't get any coffee to drink and never even tasted his cake.")

Left: Shirley
Right: Lee, Janey, and Shirley
Edna's granddaughter, circa 1931

Chapter 5 — Broad Shoulders

As Aunt Edna thought over the funny, and some not so funny, memories in her life she laughed out loud. Her mother jumped and exclaimed, "Land a mercy! What are you finding so funny? I can't find nothing funny about Janey being abandoned by her no 'count man!"

Aunt Edna interrupted, "Ma, no matter how she tells the story we both know how hardheaded Janey is. She was your baby, but you've got to admit she has always been determined to be in charge and run the show! I'm her sister and I love her truly but there's no way we could ever live together". MaMa said, "Well Edna you should turn around and head back to your home because you know exactly why she called you to come and get her." "Yeah", Aunt Edna answered, "You are right. But she's my sister and I love her despite her faults. As long as I have a biscuit, I'll share it with her."

Sarah Martha Ruark (MaMa) circa 1934

Then she laughed again, "It's your fault I'm so soft hearted. I was raised up with your rule that family should stick together because 'blood is thicker than water.' The good Lord knows I'm too old to change now."

"Yep, blame it all on me! It's all my fault!" Sarah, laughed quietly, "That's why God gave me such broad shoulders, so I could carry all the blame and guilt for whatever happens."

Like my grandmother once told my mother, "He also gave her a big bottom, so it would be easy to find when they plucked her last nerve and she was totally fed up with some stupid person disagreeing with her." The advice my grandmother gave my mother was just to storm off and mutter, "Yeh kin jest kiss meh arse!"

My mother passed that advice on to me and I'm passing it onto you. When an argument is impossible to be resolved just storm off and mutter, "Yeh kin jest kiss meh arse!"

Chapter 6 — Home-to Roost

MaMa just looked out of the car window at the countryside and wondered silently what she should say to her youngest daughter.

Aunt Edna drifted back into her silent thoughts and was trying to figure how she was going to be able to fit Mom and me in her tiny house on Short Street. She thought to herself, *"I really don't have any other choice. Janey has no place to live, no money, and no job."*

Quilt square showing Short St in orange where Sarah Martha lived, Wicomico Senior High School, the Salisbury Park and Wicomico River

She didn't want to say anything out loud to hurt her mother's feelings. But she thought silently, *"When you left Pa, you came and moved in with me. And that was O.K. We didn't quarrel about it and it turned into a good thing. When my daughter, Nina, came back home with her two children, Bobby and Joann, we needed you to help watch her little ones, so she and I could go to work at Jackson's Shirt Factory. Robert had also come with his wife, Pansy, and their daughter Shirley. Some folks have wall to wall carpet. I have wall to wall family. Because we are family, I just welcomed you all in with open arms. Then I just added a couple more potatoes and some dumplings to our supper and asked God to make a way and he has every time!"*

When Aunt Edna and MaMa arrived at Ralph's house my Mom was huddled on the front porch steps holding me in her lap and she was still crying. She fell into her mother's arms and sobbed out her woeful story. MaMa gave her youngest daughter a comforting hug and then she said "I'm real sorry, baby. But remember I told you so! You just wouldn't listen! But no one listens to me! What do I know?"

Aunt Edna's house on Short Street in Salisbury was a tight fit. She only had one bedroom upstairs, a small kitchen with a living room downstairs, and a bathroom down the path. They managed to make it work for two years somehow.

Chapter 7 — Hen's Teeth

After such close quarters in her sister's house and no sign or hope of getting a job Mom started thinking about trying her luck up the road in Wilmington. Her mother and her older sister tried to discourage her but the more they tried the more determined she became!

Again, I was listening to Mom talking to Aunt Edna, "There are no jobs for women here on the Shore because of this depression. I need a job to help put food on our table. I appreciate how much you all have helped me. But I can't continue taking advantage of you. You've got your hands full now!" Aunt Edna tried to interrupt, but Mom kept on. She said, "I've heard our president Franklin Delano Roosevelt met with Stalin from Russia and Winston Churchill from England. They decided to become allies known as The Big Three. Roosevelt did not want our country to be directly involved. Those three also knew America was in a great depression with no jobs and no money. It was decided our country would make and sell military supplies to our two allies. We needed to create more jobs in this country to get out of this depression. Hopefully the demand for more war plants will bring jobs to Wilmington."

When Mom stopped for breath, Aunt Edna said, "It sounds like a workable plan. But where will you live?"

Mom even had an answer for that! "I figure when I get a job and have money in my pocket, I shouldn't have a problem finding a place to live."

MaMa joined in, "Sounds like a plan except if all those people from the Shore go up to Wilmington to get good jobs they've probably rent all those places. Yep, all them houses you are talking about are probably scarce as hen's teeth!"

Chapter 8 – Fred Settling Down

MaMa had just returned from the grocery store to find her youngest son, Fred, resting back in her rocker with his feet propped up on the railing of Aunt Edna's porch. MaMa hollered loudly," Get your feet off of that railing!"

"Oh Ma… " Fred began.

She interrupted, "Don't you start in Ma-ing me! I mean it! I just painted them railings for Edna yesterday! Get your feet down!"

Fred stood up quickly. But he just couldn't resist teasing her as he always had. He gave a little wolf whistle as his mother grabbed the handrail and pulled herself up the steps. Loving to get her riled up he continued, "Hey, pretty lady. How are you doing?" Laughing loudly, he gave her an affectionate hug.

Returning his laughter, she brushed him off and said, "Don't you start any of your 'pretty lady nonsense'. As to how I'm feeling, I'm still standing upright. So, I reckon I'm fine! I know you are here because you want something. What is it this time?" They both shared a loud laugh. Fred had a way with all the ladies especially his mother. He always loved to get her in a jolly mood before he asked for any favors.

Then MaMa noticed the pretty little girl standing beside him. She had watched their verbal exchange in awe. She had moved down to the first step on the porch when they first started what sounded like a real argument brewing. Since they were both still laughing, she supposed everything was all right. She went back up the steps and hugged Fred. He had warned her earlier his folks were a little strange, but they were a tight knit family.

"Oh," he said "this is my sweetheart Katherin. We're planning on getting married this Friday at the courthouse and we'd really love to have you come and stand as our witness."

"Well tarnation! It doesn't seem like you are a grown-up man already. But truthfully I was beginning to think you would never take the plunge." She looked at Katherin and said, "Of course I'll be right proud to be your witness if you really want me to."

"Oh yes, I really do want you to approve of this wedding." answered Katherin. "I love Fred and he's told me how close you both are. I'm really looking forward to becoming a member of your family."

"Well, I don't know about the last part after you get to know us. But I'd sure love to be there to see this young man get married and settled down at last."

MaMa turned and spoke to her son, "You know I'm sure they'll marry you at the courthouse without me because you are a grown up now. I was beginning to think you would never think about taking on such a big responsibility."

Turning to Katherin she continued, "Are you sure you want me to be at your wedding?"

Katherin answered, "Of course we do! My mother and father have agreed to our getting married. But we really want you to be there, Mrs. Ruark." She laughed and added, "You can be my bridesmaid and hold my flowers."

Fred gave a hearty laugh and added, "Well then, everything is settled now!" Fred asked excitedly "Ain't she a beauty?"

Thinking he was talking about Katherin, MaMa gave her a big hug and said, "She sure is and you better take good care of her." Then she realized he was pointing to the shiny new car parked at the curb. "My goodness she looks expensive. She ain't yours, is she?"

"Yep, actually mine and the bank! Katherin and I are going to settle down and raise chickens and children. We plan on

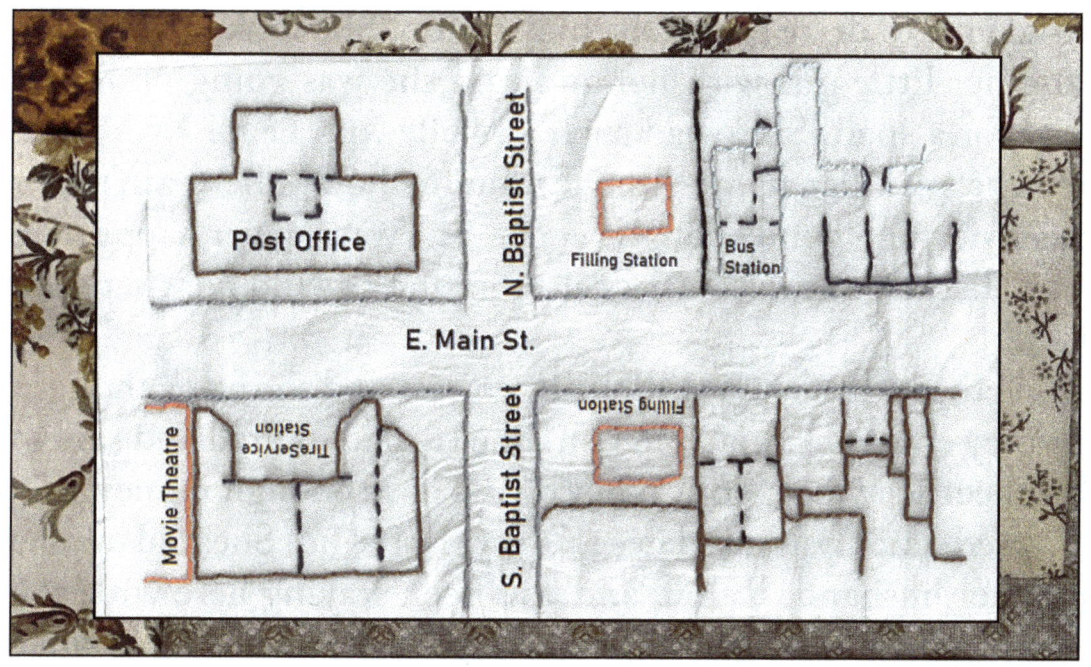

Quilt square of Salisbury map showing bus station, post office, tire service station, and various warehouses in 1936

making enough money on my chickens to pay for my car and my children." He laughed again, "If the chickens don't pan out, I guess we could move in here with you and my big sister, Edna."

This gave MaMa time for a silent pause, *"I don't know what Edna would think about you both moving in with her!"* Then she spoke out loud, "You know your big-hearted sister. She'd never expect you to live in your car as long as she's got a roof over her head!" Then she turned to Katherin and said, "Land sakes child. You must be hungry! Come on in. Edna's got some chicken and dumplings left from last night's supper. It'll take just a jiffy to warm some up."

Then she asked Fred, "Did you see Janey?"

He answered, "Yep, she came out of the house just as we drove up. She was wearing her fancy church clothes and she asked me to drive her to the bus station. She took her suitcase and her little girl with her and said she was going up to the city for a spell. She's had such a swelled-up head! Ever since Pa changed her name from Emma to Janey there ain't ever been nothing good enough for her. She wasn't ever happy here in Salisbury anyway. Guess she's gonna try and be what she's not!"

MaMa was always the family worrier and she had a thought as they entered Edna's kitchen. She turned to Fred and said in a concerned voice, "But Janey didn't have enough money!"

Fred quickly assured her. "Oh yeah she did! She told me she left her husband, Ralph, and had been staying here with you and Edna for the last two years. She also told me she had some money she made picking blueberries during the past summer. You know she's always been stingy enough to hold onto a nickel until the buffalo bellers!" Then he leaned down and whispered quietly. "Oh, that reminds me I've been meaning to ask you for something. Could you spare me a little money for me to get a ring and some flowers for Katherin?"

MaMa answered in a quiet voice, "I knew you wanted something else when you asked me to come to your wedding."

Chapter 9 — Riding the Greyhound

After PaPa changed my Mom's name from Emma to Janey all the Ruark family called her Janey. But to me she has always been my Mom.

She didn't bother looking back out of the bus window now. She had made her decision. *"My suitcase is tucked under my seat. My baby, Violetta, is safe and secure on my lap. I have all I own and all I need in the world right here!"* She silently thought, *"Well I can't change my mind now! I am on the bus and on my way to Wilmington!"* Still thinking she wondered, *"I sure hope this is the right decision. Well, no sense worrying about it! I'll just have to wait and see. If I need to worry, I can wait and worry tomorrow."*

She drifted off to sleep soundly and only woke up as the bus was pulling into the Wilmington bus depot. Gathering up her coat and suitcase she held onto my hand tightly and silently prayed, *"Lord, stay by our side. There's so much confusion and so many people!"*

She had not really planned past getting to Wilmington. She laughed, looked at me, and said, "Now what?" She looked across the busy street and saw the answer to her question. There was a large sign in one of the windows,

St. Peter's Jesus in courtyard dedicated in 1928 Picture taken in 2019

"Rooms for Rent." She walked with confidence toward her future. An old scary looking man said gruffly, "We don't rent to anyone with kids here!" Mom quickly showed him some money and said, "This is my daughter, Violetta. She is a very quiet child and this money should be enough to help you change your mind!" He mumbled quickly, "Well I guess I can let you stay for a week or two if you keep her quiet!"

After we got settled in Mom decided it would be a good idea for us to take a short walk around the neighborhood and get 'the lay of the land' as my PaPa used to say.

St. Peter's courtyard in 2019

Chapter 10 — Saint Peter's Church

The first thing Mom and I saw looked like a grand castle where a king might live. After reading the large sign by the front door she said, "It's a Catholic church." Now she wasn't Catholic. She told me what Aunt Edna, had said when she learned about her little sister's idea of going to Wilmington.

Mom said, "I can almost hear her now, 'Janey, when you get there don't act like you just got off the boat!'"

I could tell now Mom had a plan. I watched her as she "patted herself up" as my MaMa used to say. After making sure her hair was neat and her clothes not too wrinkled, we walked in through those huge front doors. Inside it was so beautiful with pretty colored glass windows going clear up to the ceiling. We heard soft friendly music as we entered. There in the middle of this big room was a huge statue of Jesus. He was standing with his arms spread wide as though he was welcoming us in. He looked just like the picture my MaMa had hanging on the wall in her bedroom in Salisbury. I felt less afraid when I saw it, but I still held my Mom's hand as tight as I could.

Chapter 11 — New Friends

I didn't know much about Catholics and what I had heard from family members wasn't very good. I knew all us Ruarks were supposed to be Baptist. But none of us ever went to the Baptist church except MaMa and me.

A smiling lady in a long black dress came up to us and shook Mom's hand. She was wearing a funny white hat. It reminded me of those big old sea gulls who spread their wings so wide when they flew around the beach back home. Anyway, she and Mom talked in whispers like they had a secret. Then she took us into another room and told us to take a chair and she left.

I didn't know why or where she wanted us to take a chair, so I just watched Mom sit down. Then I climbed up on her lap and we waited, and we waited. Just as I was beginning to relax a large door burst open and a tall man with a big friendly smile came into the room. He was also dressed in a long black dress like the lady had worn. He had a necklace of beads around his waist with a tiny statue of Jesus fastened to it. But he didn't have one of those big bird hats on his head. He told us his name was Father Daugherty and he apologized for keeping us waiting so long. He said he had been in a mess. Mom later explained he had been in a mass which was something like our church services back on the Shore. He gave me some paper and a pencil. I sat at his big desk, drew some pictures, and pretended to write about our trip to Wilmington.

They were talking very softly, but I heard Mom say we had just arrived in the city. Then she told him we were staying in the "Rooms to Rent" place. She also told him she wanted to study and learn to be a good Catholic and she wanted me to go to Catholic school and be raised in the Catholic faith. I thought silently, *"Nope, Nope!"* I remember hearing her tell

Aunt Edna the first thing she would do in Wilmington was get someone to take care of me, so she could get a job. I didn't say it out loud now though because she had taught me as far back as I could remember if she ever said anything not true to anyone, I should never correct her. She even explained it might be necessary to tell one of her little white lies to keep us safe sometime.

Father Daugherty was a believer and he believed everything Mom said. He put his hand on my head and said, "Bless you my child." He was getting me mixed up. I wasn't his child! Then he and Mom bowed their heads and said a prayer. I just whispered the Lord's Prayer which MaMa had taught me. It was the only prayer I knew. Then Mom and I went back to our room in the "Rooms to Rent" place. She told me Father Daugherty had volunteered to be my godfather. She explained the best part was she would not have to pay anything for me to go to Saint Peter's Catholic School.

I guess it would be nice to have a father even if he did wear a dress. I knew I must have had a real father some time. But Mom had told me not to talk about him and I never did.

Chapter 12 — Terribly Sick

We went back to see Father Daugherty the next day and he enrolled me in their Catholic preschool. Mom was still looking for a job and she left me there with a lady who wanted me to call her Sister Theresa. I was getting even more mixed up because I knew she wasn't my sister, but she was awfully nice.

Mom really did try but she wasn't able to find a job. I went to preschool every day and she went looking and asking. She told me there just wasn't any work to be had. Her blueberry money had run out. We had no money left to buy food. I was alright because I got breakfast and lunch at school. I didn't know it, but Mom just did without and after a while she got awful sick. School was only a block away. One day she was so sick she couldn't even get out of bed to walk with me to school. I was sitting in a chair beside her bed trying to figure out what to do when I heard a knock at the door of our room.

Violetta in St. Peter's uniform with school in background circa 1938

Two of those Catholic sisters from the school came in. They wanted to know why I was still home. Sister Theresa got me dressed and walked me to school. Sister Margaret stayed with Mom the whole day except when she went to the school lunchroom and got her some soup. Sister Theresa told Father Daugherty about Mom being so sick.

He walked me home after school. There I sat on the floor, put some paper on one of the chairs we had, and pretended to be writing more about our adventures in Wilmington. He sat beside Mom's bed in our other chair and they had another very long and quiet talk.

    I wondered if everyone in Wilmington always whispered. But after this we met Mom Toso and she sure didn't whisper! She talked fast and loud more like our Ruark family.

Chapter 13 — A Good Friend

Father Daugherty arranged a meeting with Mom Toso the very next day. She was a member of his church and a good friend. Surprisingly, Mom accepted her offer to come live with her for a little while.

Mom Toso took us on a tour of her house. It was bright, cheerful and very clean. There was a faint smell like fresh cut lemons everywhere. She had fixed up a beautiful room for us. There was a tiny bird sitting in a cage. It was singing a happy song. A large bed with a pretty quilt was in one of the corners of the room for Mom and me to share. A fancy desk was in another corner where I could practice printing the A B C s we were learning at school. There was a radio sitting on a table in the third corner. Mom Toso told us we could hear stories and news of the war in Germany or just enjoy some music from it. The grandest thing of all was in the fourth corner. Mom Toso's son, Maurice, had brought up from their basement the largest doll house I had ever seen. In fact, it was the only one I had ever seen! There were three little dolls to be the mother, father, and a little girl just like me. Each room had tiny doll furniture in it. Mom Toso told me it had been her daughters when she was little like me. I had never been so happy in my whole life. I felt as though I would just burst!

The next day Mom and I moved into Mom Toso's house. I was so glad because I didn't like our "Rooms to Rent" place. It was dirty and dark, and it smelled stinky like old cabbage and spoiled fish.

We ate spaghetti and meatballs on the first night at Mom Toso's. It was quite a treat for me. I had never eaten spaghetti before. It was so delicious, and she put so much on my plate. I tried to make her happy and eat it all. My tummy just couldn't hold it. I asked her if she could keep it for me for breakfast in the morning. I told her when we lived with my MaMa down on the Shore she often said, "Food always tasted better when it was heated again in the morning!" Sometimes we would have something extra good for breakfast like warmed up ham and cabbage. We might even have pork chops with gravy and mashed potatoes.

Mom Toso laughed, pulled me into her welcoming lap, and hugged me so tight I could barely breathe. "Oh, you little angel," she said, "We'll have something even better for breakfast!"

So much was happening I couldn't get to sleep. I tossed most of the night and wondered, "What could possibly be better than spaghetti and meatballs?"

In the morning, I woke to the smell of sweet warm cinnamon rolls. I jumped out of bed and thought I must surely be in heaven. After breakfast, Mom and Mom Toso lingered over their coffee while I played under the table. I'm sure they didn't even notice I was there. Mom Toso said Father Daugherty's congregation had been wonderful to her family when they first arrived.

"Luckily", she said, "my husband was able to get me, our son, Maurice, and my little girl out of Italy before Mussolini made it impossible for anyone to leave." She talked a little bit about how

Mom Toso's house in Wilmington Picture taken in 2019

awful it had been. A lot of her friends and family were starting to disappear in both Germany and Italy. Then she began to cry softly when she confessed, she worried that she would never see any of the rest of her family alive again. "What a relief to safely be in America!" Her husband had left her a lot of money when he died. To honor his memory and in gratitude to her adopted country, she was happy to help people who were less fortunate. I guessed she meant people like Mom and me.

Chapter 14 — Liar! Liar!

They made a funny pair, Mom Toso and Maurice. She was tiny and always wore a black dress, like a little blackbird. He was tall and well-fed and loved brightly colored ties. He reminded me a lot of my Uncle Fred who would rather tease someone than eat when they were hungry.

Her daughter was grown, married and living in another city and she was dearly missed. I think that's why she was so happy to have Mom and me there. She wasn't alone because her son, Maurice, lived with her but still, I heard her tell Mom, a son is not the same as a daughter.

Mom was still weak and rested a lot. Mom Toso had a special dessert she would only give to my mom. Maurice and I were not allowed to have any. We had cake or pie and ice cream, so I really didn't mind at all. Mom Toso said her pudding would help Mom get better quickly. It must have been working because Mom's cheeks were getting a rosier color. She wasn't as tired as she was before we moved in.

One night after another delicious dinner, Maurice and Mom were sitting in the living room listening to the radio. Mom Toso let me listen to the Bob Hope, Jack Benny, or Fibber McKee shows. They were listening to a radio program called Inner Sanctum and she said it was too scary. She was letting me help her with the dishes, so I didn't care.

"Liar! Liar! Liar!" We heard Mom scream. Mom Toso and I ran into the living room and saw her stretched out on the couch. She was crying! I had never seen Mom cry before. She said Maurice had told her his mother had been feeding her blood pudding.

Mom Toso turned on Maurice and said, "Testa Dura! Hard head! You shut upah you face! I'm ah gonnah slappah you aside ofah you head!" And she did! She always had a tea towel tucked into the waist of her apron. I never knew why until now. Whack! Whack! She could reach him easily with it and she was very accurate. Then she said a whole lot more, most of it in Italian. But I was sent to our room and was not able to hear the rest. Mom explained it to me later. Maurice was jealous of my Mom because of all the extra attention, so he told Mom her special dessert was blood pudding. Mom Toso explained it was commonly used in the "old country". Mom said she understood and was grateful for her care and concern but there was no more blood pudding offered or eaten. Mom was much better anyway so it must've done the trick.

Chapter 15 – Alike but Different

Mom Toso was like my MaMa in a lot of ways. They both knew some strange old-fashioned remedies to cure different sicknesses. She admitted the pudding was really made of blood from beef livers. It was a medical remedy her grandmother in Italy had taught her. She knew it would help Mom get well. It did! But Mom never ate pudding at Mom Toso's again!

MaMa didn't make any Italian blood pudding. She knew though if you got run down and weak you should eat a lot of chicken livers cooked rare. Many years later when I was fifteen, I got very sick and weak. Doctor Sohler, our family doctor, told my Mom to feed me chicken livers cooked with bacon. He said it had to be cooked rare because my blood was too thin. She did, and I got well very quickly. I wondered if he was taught that by his grandmother from the old country.

Mom Toso reminded me a lot of my MaMa back home on the Shore. She said some of her words kind of funny like MaMa, but in a different way. I soon learned she was also like MaMa because she was soft to hug. Her lap was the best place to be whenever I was hurt or scared. Her hair was twisted up like a bun on the back of her head just like MaMas. But hers was black as a crow flying in a dark night and MaMa's was white as snow. Mom Toso lived in a mansion. MaMa lived in Aunt Edna's little house you could fit inside Mom Toso's living room and kitchen.

They were both built the same. PaPa

Sarah Martha (MaMa) at the farm

used to laugh and say, "Saree's low to the ground and round!" For many years I used to imagine all the angels in heaven who watched over little children were built the same way. They would neither one put up with a lot of nonsense. But they both had the same twinkle in their eyes and laughed a lot. Both had a heart bigger than a barrel and were wonderful in the kitchen but with entirely different foods.

MaMa's specialty was Southern foods like chicken and dumplings, sweet potato biscuits, corn pone, or hush puppies. Mom Toso would win hands down with her Italian foods like spaghetti and meatballs, lasagna, fettucine, or ravioli.

They both made everything from scratch. Neither one could ever give you a recipe. They both measured with a pinch of this, a dash of that, and a scoop of something else.

Chapter 16 — Another New Friend

Mom and I both liked staying with Mom Toso and her son. Mom was now looking much better and a lot stronger. She went to look for a job, so we could start paying our own way. She was lucky and got a job up town at a five and dime store called Woolworths. She was the happiest I had seen her in a long time. She was so excited. At supper that night she told us the next thing she planned to do was to find a real home. She told Mom Toso how much we both loved living with her but she really believed we should be getting on with our lives. Caught up in Mom's excitement, Mom Toso said she had a friend, Charles Bartoleane. He owned a barber shop just up the street on West Seventh Street. It was only a block from her house. He had several houses he rented out. She suggested we should visit him the next day and see if he had any available for rent.

She told Mom, "It seems like I've known Charlie my whole life. We lived in the same town in Italy. He helped arrange so my husband, our two children, and I were able to come to America. I believe he is a good man. But you still must be careful who you trust."

*Charlie's Barbershop
Picture taken in 2019*

She had a scheduled meeting with Father Daugherty and couldn't go with us. She called Mr. Bartoleane and told him to expect us around ten in the morning.

Mom said, "God must

have been smiling down on us." When she explained her interest in his rental properties Mr. Bartoleane's answer was "Yes! Indeed, I do! I have several available. The one I have in mind would be just perfect for you and your little girl!"

He continued on, "My original plan was to remodel this house and make three apartments out of it. There was to be an apartment on each floor. I'd have to put in two more kitchens and another bathroom. The building inspector told me I would have to get an electrician to put in new wiring so each of the apartments could have its own meter. I'd have to tear out the furnace in the basement and figure out how each apartment could have its own stove for heat. Whatever I did, it was going to cost way too much. It seemed like a good idea at first. But times are getting tight." He laughed loudly, shrugged his shoulders, and said, "Like everyone says we're in the middle of a depression now!" No one, including Mr. Bartoleane, had much money. Lots of his customers had lost their jobs and stopped coming to him. They were shining their own shoes and getting their shaves and haircuts at home now just like the Ruarks had always done.

Mr. Bartoleane continued, "Say, how about if I give you the keys and you can walk over there to see it now. It's not far. It's just down West Seventh Street. The number on the house is 221."

Chapter 17 — Wood Stoves and Spiders

It had snowed, and it was really cold when Mom and I went to see about maybe renting this house. I ran in excitedly. The first thing I looked for was a nice warm stove like Aunt Edna had in her living room. *"Oh Oh! There wasn't a stove of any kind!"* Right away I thought, *"I don't think I want to live here."*

We had lived down on the Shore with Aunt Edna and MaMa before coming to Wilmington. There was a big wood stove standing on the floor in the living room. When it was really cold, we'd just crowd up close to it. Then we'd be warm as a grilled cheese sandwich frying in a skillet. None of Aunt Edna's other rooms had a woodstove. When it was time for bed we'd put on our flannel nighties and just fly upstairs as fast as we could. It was so cold! Once we were under all those quilts on her bed it was plenty warm. But they were so heavy I couldn't even turn over!

We walked quickly through this house. I was surprised to see there were three floors. It had not one, but two bathrooms and they were both inside! I told Mom I didn't want to live in a house as cold all over as Aunt Edna's hall and bedroom. She just laughed and said, "Oh, don't worry honey. There's a big stove in the basement."

Well, first of all, I didn't know what a basement was. Mom

Sarah (MaMa) on steps of her house

opened a door in the kitchen, held my hand and we walked down some creaky stairs into a nasty dark room. She found a string hanging from the ceiling. She pulled it and a dim light came on. "This is the basement and that's our stove!"

"No! No!" I decided quickly. I didn't want to come down here and huddle around such a nasty old stove no matter how big it was! There were even cobwebs everywhere. And where there are cobwebs it means there will be spiders too. Aunt Edna didn't have a basement under her house and she didn't have spiders either. Now I was sure. I did not want Mom to rent this house! My mind was made up. I knew right away I wanted to go back home to Salisbury and stay with my MaMa!

Chapter 18 — Great Potential

When Mom saw Mr. Bartoleane's vacant house on Seventh Street she also saw it's potential. She went back to his barbershop for a talk with him. She gave him the idea of her renting his whole house just like it was. He agreed to accept her rent as a deposit and sell her the house at the end of one year. He liked her idea because he wouldn't have to spend any money he didn't have. They agreed on the amount of rent, the final purchase price, and the date of the purchase. Then they found a lawyer to write up the lease and contract. Mom told me those papers would make it all legal and binding just as though her Pa had shaken his hand on their agreement. Mom said the house wouldn't really be ours until she paid off the mortgage at the bank. I didn't understand what a mortgage was. But I prayed every night and cried real tears too hoping she wouldn't be able to pay off whatever a mortgage thing was. I didn't like the big ugly stove or the dark basement with the creaky stairs. I really wanted to go back down to my MaMa's on the Shore. As Mom so often reminded me she was the boss. It didn't take us very long to move into our new home. We only had the one suitcase we brought with us to Wilmington.

Janey (Mom) in Wilmington

Chapter 19 — Another Schemer

Remember Uncle Fred was my mother's brother. MaMa called him a schemer. She called my Mom a dreamer because she wanted so much. Well I think my Mom was a schemer too.

Mom had a plan all thought out as soon as she saw Mr. Bartoleane's house. She went to a furniture store and talked the salesman into letting her have two beds with two sets of sheets and two pillows on credit. She also got a few dishes, a pot, a frying pan, and a small kitchen table with two chairs. He gave her a nice flashlight too. He said she could use it until we got our electric turned on. I think she could have talked him out of his shoelaces if she had a use for them.

The next thing she did was put one of those "Room for Rent" signs in our front window. Mom's sign wasn't in the window very long when two men came knocking on the door at the same time.

She had figured she'd only get one roomer and he could have one bed in one room. She told me we could share the other room and bed. But now she had two roomers and a bed for each of them. Where would Mom and I sleep?

Kevin and Earnest each offered to pay for their rooms a week in advance. They had their cash in hand and Mom couldn't let either one of them get away. So, she let each one have his own room with his own bed on the second floor.

221 W. 7th Street in Wilmington, 2019 Notice the patch in the sidewalk where the grate used to be.

Chapter 20 — Camping Out

Now there was no bed left for Mom and me. We locked the door to a room downstairs and made our bed on the floor with our coats. Mom said we could pretend we were camping out in the woods like her brother Fred used to do when he was little. We talked and giggled a lot before we went to sleep.

Mom went back to the furniture man early the next day and paid him the one roomer's money on her bill. He was glad to see her so soon with money. He never even blinked when she said she would need one more bed and two sheets and two pillows. We kept this for ourselves and put them in our bedroom downstairs.

The other roomer's money was used to get our electric and gas turned on. It was good to have electric because the flashlight the furniture man gave Mom didn't give enough light to see much. And with the gas for our kitchen stove Mom could cook our food which she had also bought.

Map Legend
This is a small quilted street map of the Wilmington area described in the book. The gray strips represent streets.

On the lower left, you can see Charlie's Barbershop and Jeanie's boarding house on W. 7th Street. Up the block and on the other side of W. 7th Street is St Peters Cathedral and school. Top right shows Mom Toso's house on N. West Street. These buildings and streets still exist today but you must look hard to recognize them.

Chapter 21 — Second Week's Rent

A week later when the two men paid their rent again Mom took their money to the furniture man to pay for the stuff, he gave her on credit. She also used part of it to buy a bureau for each of her two roomers. She told me they needed a place to put their clothes. She used what was left to get some more food for us.

She called her sister, Edna, and asked her to come up for a visit and see what she was doing in the city. "Oh, by the way," she added, "Look around and see if you have any curtains or curtain material, towels, and wash clothes in good shape. Please box them up and bring them with you." The next time Mom got her rent money she went back to the furniture man. She bought three blankets and finished paying off her bill.

A year had passed. Mom was very busy, and time seemed to pass quickly. She was still 'talking a good game,' as her Pa used to say. She explained she had to go to the bank and get her money to pay Mr. Bartoleane. The bank man paid him for his house. Mom got her papers which she called our mortgage. Now, whether I liked it or not, our house belonged to us and the bank.

Mom really got to like Mr. Bartoleane. She told me I should call him Uncle Charlie. And I did. He came to our house a lot in his long black car. The man who drove him to our house was called his chauffeur. His name was Tony and he always slept outside in the car when Uncle Charlie came to visit overnight.

With her rent coming in, Mom soon had four nicely furnished rooms for her four roomers on the second and third floor. They had to take turns using the one bathroom. Downstairs Mom and I had a living room, kitchen, two bedrooms, and a private bathroom for us. She made very strict rules for the people who rented her rooms. There was to be no drinking, no women, lights were out at ten, no smoking and no hot plate cooking in their rooms. They knew she meant what she said. I think Mom really liked being the boss.

Everyone began to call her Mom except Pop DelaRosa. He was a much older man, with no job, snow white hair, and no money to pay rent with. They came to an agreement where he could have a room and his meals free if he would do all the cleaning, washing clothes, and doing the dishes. Their business talk ended with him saying. "I'mah gonnah callah you Missa Jeanie because I'mah too oldah to callah you Mom ah. That's o.k.?"

"Yes, and I'll call you Pop," she answered. She told me I would have to call the other roomers Mr. and add their first name. She said I should call Pop by his whole name Pop DelaRosa.

Things had settled down now and our group at Mom's rooming house had become like one big family almost like the Ruarks back home in Salisbury.

Chapter 22 — A Bigger Pocket Book

Aunt Edna had taught Mom to be a very good cook. When her roomers came in to pay their rent, they told Mom the smell of the food made them homesick and hungry. They all ate in restaurants and they hated it. They said it smelled awful and tasted worse. Mom told Pop DelaRosa to put some more plates and food on the table. The renters didn't have enough chairs, so they just sat cross legged on the floor and happily finished off their feast. When they were full, they got up groaning with satisfaction to go to their rooms. They each put some money on the table. Mom protested weakly she couldn't take their money. They all said it was the best meal they had since they came to Wilmington. Mr. Jack asked in a joking way if her restaurant would be open tomorrow. "Of course!" she laughed. After they were out of hearing distance Pop DelaRosa asked, "Missa Jeanie, are you gonnah feedah them every night?"

"Sure," she answered. "I'll just add another potato and some more dumplin's to the pot."

He just sighed, "You crazy lady Missa Jeanie and your heart she'sah too big!"

I laughed silently, and I thought, *"Mom's gonna need a bigger pocketbook too!"*

Chapter 23 — The Little Racketeer

Mr. Ernest, one of Mom's boarders, had just got off his shift at work. He came up the front steps where I was sitting looking bored and wishing I had something to do. Seeing my sad face, he changed his mind, went back down the steps and down the street. In a few minutes he was back again. He bought me a brand-new comic book from the book rack in Uncle Charlie's barber shop. It was about a superhero named, Superman. Mr. Earnest said, "Maybe you can give me a smile now."

"Wow!" Of course, I could smile! I smiled from ear to ear. 'Just like a possum chewing on an old yeller jacket!' as MaMa and PaPa used to say.

That's how I became something of a schemer like my Mom and her brother, Fred. From that time on about once or twice a week when one of Mom's boarders would come home, they'd see me sitting on the front steps with a pitiful look on my face. I had practiced it in my mirror until I got it just right. I would get another brand-new comic book and I would brighten right up just like a 'crow in a corn field'. At supper one night Mom gave all of the boarders a short lecture about spoiling me. They all protested and said it wasn't a big deal. It was worth a dime to buy a comic book just to see me smile!

Violetta and toy dog, Fala, in front of 221 W. 7th Street circa 1942
Notice the grate which is now cemented over.

I had the best comic book collection in the area. There was Captain Marvel, Batman and Green Lantern etc. After I read them, I kept them on the shelves in my bedroom. I rented them out to my friends in the neighborhood for a week at the bargain price of a nickel each. If they returned the comic book in good condition, they could rent another one. Mom's roomers paid for all my comic books. I saved the money I rented them out for and bought lots of great stuff from the Newberry dime store up town. I once heard Uncle Charlie laughing and telling Mom she was raising a little racketeer and his comic book business was booming.

Chapter 24 — A New Game

It was summer. Aunt Katherin and Uncle Fred came to visit us in Wilmington on a weekend. They asked Mom if I could go back home with them to visit and play with their baby girl, Nancy. It should have been fun, but it turned out to be very scary.

Aunt Katherin and Uncle Fred had a house out in the middle of a big forest which was nice in the daytime. But there were strange sounds at night. I recognized some of the sounds like the crickets, the owls, and the dogs barking. But those other strange sounds were frightening to me. One night, Uncle Fred went out for a friendly game of cards with some of his friends. His baby daughter, Nancy, was asleep in her crib and Aunt Katherin had put me in her big bed to sleep with her. She had a whole lot of quilts to keep me warm and comfortable. I was safe from those strange noises in the woods. I cuddled up to her and drifted off into a deep sleep.

Then I felt Aunt Katherin's hands gently touching my lips as she whispered softly, "Sh, sh, sh. Don't make a sound. We're going to play a funny new game. You must be very quiet. You can't say a word if we want to be the winners."

Aunt Katherin was holding baby Nancy, who was sound asleep, in her arms. She was wrapped up snuggly in her baby quilt and had a molasses tit in her mouth. Her bottle was also in the pocket of Aunt Katherin's jacket. She lifted me up onto her other hip and whispered again, "Shhh, not a word, not a sound!" I knew she meant it, so I held my breath and clung tightly to her neck. She walked quickly out to Uncle Fred's truck, opened the door silently, and put me in on the driver's side. She motioned for me to slide over and gently laid Nancy on the seat between us. She silently locked my door and handed

Nancy's bottle to me. She locked her door quietly and put the key in the truck's keyhole. The truck started up with a roar!

Suddenly out of the black night two large dark shapes came running up to the truck. They jumped up on the running boards and tried to open the truck doors. They pounded on the windows with their fists. One of them yelled, "Open this door! Bitch!"

The man at my window looked like a wild animal. I remember he had an ugly face, bright red lips, large white eyes, and looked just furious like he wanted to kill us all!

The truck lurched forward and they both fell off of the running boards. We zoomed down the lane. It was a wild exciting ride and Aunt Katherin never stopped or even slowed down until we got to Aunt Edna's house in Salisbury. She grabbed both Nancy and me, ran up on the porch, and knocked loudly on the door.

MaMa quickly opened the door. Speaking loudly, she said, "What are you knocking for? You know I don't ever lock our door. You've most likely woke the whole neighborhood!" Then she began trying to get some answers.

Aunt Katherin just fell into her comforting arms. She gave me a big smile and said to MaMa, "We'll talk about it later. But right now, I need a cup of strong black coffee. We played a new game and Violetta helped me be the winner, so she needs a glass of milk and a piece of some yummy pie."

Baby Nancy was still sleeping soundly. She was put in Aunt Edna's bed with her bottle of milk. When I finished my milk and pie Aunt Katherin took me upstairs and tucked me in.

I was sleepy and as I drifted off to sleep I thought it had been a very exciting night. We had played a strange new game. I was glad we had been the winners and MaMa's pie was delicious. Sometime later I learned what had really happened. After she put me to bed Aunt Katherin told Aunt Edna and MaMa the whole horrid story how those awful men had broken into her home. She was very upset and went on to say, "All of this terrible war talk about Hitler in Germany is making everybody crazy!" Then she gave them a frightened warning, "It's a sure thing. From now on everybody is going to have to lock and bolt all of their doors or get murdered in their sleep!"

(This event helped me better understand the importance of children paying attention and doing what they are told with no arguing or questioning. It did save my life and it might save yours someday.)

Fred, Johnny, Katherin, Francis, Sarah (MaMa), Lee (PaPa), Nancy, and Violetta many years after the "New Game"

Chapter 25 — Scary Times

I really wasn't old enough to understand why all the grown-ups everywhere were always talking about this horrible war overseas.

MaMa had told me about the wise old owl a long time ago. She had told me, "The more he heard the less he spoke and the less he spoke the more he learned!" I became a very good listener and I learned a lot. I still remember when Mom and I went to the movies there was always a short news reel movie showing Hitler and the atrocities he caused. It was very, very scary! Hitler's latest victim was Great Britain. The people there were suffering nightly bombings with many casualties. His plan was to conquer the whole world. A few wise people began to think we should begin to prepare for this mad man's invasion just to be sure.

War talk or not Aunt Katherin wouldn't go back to their house even to get her things. She refused to ever live way out in the country again. Uncle Fred and she squeezed into Aunt Edna's small house on Short Street in Salisbury until he could get a house built up on Ruark Drive. It was very close to Uncle Johnny's brown bungalow on Zion Road. She wouldn't be scared anymore because as MaMa said, "Now Johnny and Frances could come running to help if Katherin just gave them a loud holler!"

Chapter 26 — My Christmas Lesson

Aunt Edna's boy, Norman, was out of school for the Christmas break. He had come up to Wilmington to spend a few days with Mom and me. I loved him like a big brother, but I couldn't understand why he liked to tease me so much just to make me cry. Sometimes he was so sweet to me and other times he was just awful! Mom told me her brother Fred used to do the same thing to her. She said, "Sweetie, he's just a boy and that's what boys do. Hopefully he'll grow out of it."

I thought this visit had been the best ever. But just before he left to go back down to the Shore with his mother he told me there was no Santa Claus! Of course, I cried. Then he started teasing me and calling me a big baby because I still believed in Santa Claus. I was so mad with him and really glad when he had to go back to Salisbury with his mother for the rest of the school Christmas holidays.

Uncle Charlie brought us the biggest and the most beautiful Christmas tree I ever saw. A few nights later he came by and helped us trim it with some tinsel, brightly colored lights, and other decorations. Now it was the night before Christmas. I couldn't go to sleep even if I tried. I was trying to stay awake and catch Santa coming in with my presents. That would prove Norman was wrong! I thought I heard someone in the living room, so I crawled silently out of my bed and tiptoed across the hall. Then I hid behind the door to the living room and listened. I didn't hear any jolly "Ho, Ho, Ho's".

All I could hear was Uncle Charlie and Mom's voices. I could hear but I had to see for myself! Very quietly and quickly I took a chance and looked! Norman was right! There really was no Santa Claus!

I saw Uncle Charlie and Mom putting presents under our

Violetta circa 1940

Christmas tree. I sat and watched quietly until they were finished. I saw him kiss Mom and then I crept silently back to bed. I was so disappointed I really couldn't go to sleep now.

I tossed and turned the rest of the night and finally fell asleep as the sun was coming up. Mom came in and playfully tickled my nose," Well, sleepy head, are you going to sleep all day? It's Christmas you know!"

Mom had made a special Christmas breakfast of waffles. I loved waffles but for some reason I couldn't swallow them. I just pushed my food around on my plate and pretended to eat. There weren't any of the usual happy sounds of surprise as we opened our presents.

Mom sensed something was wrong and put me on her lap. After a big hug and kiss she asked me why I was so sad on Christmas day. I told her what Norman had said about there being no Santa Claus. "Oh, sweetie, you know Norman is a lot like my, brother Fred. He'd rather tease than eat even if he was starving! You shouldn't pay much attention to anything Norman says. Of course, there is a Santa Claus!"

I sobbed, "But I saw you and Uncle Charlie putting our presents under our tree!" My quick-thinking Mom said, "Oh silly, silly, silly, you! Of course, there's a Santa Claus! Norman was probably just upset because Santa knew he had stopped believing in him. When you stop believing Santa stops coming." That sounded possible, but I still wasn't satisfied. "What about you and Uncle Charlie putting the presents under our tree?" I asked.

She answered "Oh, honey, you know it's impossible for anyone, even a super Santa Claus, to go to all the homes of all the children who believe in him. So, he asks people like Uncle Charlie to make some deliveries for him. Remember though you must believe, or Santa Claus will stop coming and he will not ask anyone to deliver presents to you. In fact, if you noticed I got some nice presents too this year!"

(Like I tell my grandchildren today, "I am eighty-six years old now, I still believe in Santa Claus and I always find at least one present under the tree for me!" Then with a wink I always add, "So you should just keep on believing!")

Chapter 27 — Slight Misunderstanding

Mom seemed very happy knowing Mr. Bartoleane and he was real nice to her. After they made their agreement about her buying his house he came to visit a lot. Mom told me I should call him Uncle Charlie. I didn't think he liked kids though because he was only nice to me when Mom was around. He didn't like it because when he wanted to take Mom someplace she always insisted I should go with them. She didn't know anyone she could get to take care of me.

Uncle Charlie wasn't very happy, but he let me tag along so she would go with him. I must admit even if he didn't seem to like me much he always brought me a pretty dress to wear. He bought some for Mom too. He even got her some beautiful jewelry. She let me play with it when he wasn't at our house. Mom always dressed very nicely and made me wear one of those silly frilly dresses Uncle Charlie bought for me. We never got to do much fun stuff though. Usually he just took us out to dinner. He didn't like any places close to our house. Tony, his chauffeur, always drove a long distance in another town to a fancy restaurant which Uncle Charlie preferred. Mom had always warned me to be seen and not heard and to use good manners. I remember Tony brought me some crayons and a book I could color in so Mom and Uncle Charlie could talk without me butting in too much. It was very boring for me. I tried hard to please Uncle Charlie because he was so good to Mom, but I remember one time when I totally embarrassed him.

We were in this fancy restaurant. It was very quiet there. There was no loud talking like the Ruarks did at dinner. There was a very large black man who stood right beside our table. He was wearing a suit like I had seen men wear at a wedding back home. Mom quietly explained his job was to get the foods we wanted from the kitchen and he was called a waiter. This seemed strange to me because down on the Shore MaMa cooked the food and then brought it to everyone at her table.

The waiter man brought our salad. Mom and Uncle Charlie weren't paying any attention to me. They were busy talking and didn't hear me when I spoke up. I had been told to speak softly like a lady and I did. First, I said it softly, "Mom! Bing Ninger. They just ignored me, so I repeated it a little louder, Bing Ninger!" They kept right on talking so I said it even louder, "Bing Ninger, Mommy Bing..!" She tried to shush me. But I refused to hush. I just got louder! Our waiter began to look like he was getting mad. Mom and Uncle Charlie still paid no attention to me. So, I repeated it a little louder, "Mom! Bing Ninger! Bing Ninger!" They kept right on talking so I repeated it as loud as I could, "Mom! Bing Ninger! Bing Ninger." I became angry because they kept talking. Finally, I just threw my fork on the floor! Mom's face got really red like it did whenever she was embarrassed. She quickly said to Uncle Charlie, "Oh Honey, she's trying to say vinegar! She wants some on her salad!" Our waiter brought the vinegar. Now he was smiling broadly. I was happy and so was everyone else.

Chapter 28 – Helping the F.B.I.

Uncle Charlie came for another visit and I overheard him telling Mom he had some friends who were F.B.I. agents and they needed to set up a base headquarters in Wilmington. They wanted a place which wouldn't attract any attention. Mom's location would be perfect to set up their phone taps and maintain surveillance which would give them useful information to track down any German spies in our area. He told her she would be helping protect our country and besides they made her a money offer she couldn't refuse. He also warned her not to tell anyone who they were or what they were planning. She liked his idea and the money too! She got ambitious and cleaned our basement out and scrubbed it down. She even got some large buckets of whitewash and painted the floors, the walls, and the ceiling too.

Some rough looking men came in carrying a big toolbox, a very long table, and some large bundles of wire. They also had a big box full of telephones. The neighbor kids were all curious and asked me what was going on. I honestly didn't know and so I couldn't tell them anything. One of the men couldn't resist teasing and he joked with us saying, "Yep this big basement will make a great place to keep our German Shepherds!" Another man told us sternly we were not to ever go in the basement because one of the German Shepherds in there would get awful fierce. He told us this one was really bad, and he would attack anyone who tried to get in. So, we never tried. We would hear a fierce scratching noise on the basement door once in a while. We decided to stay far away from all of those German Shepherds, especially the one who was so mean!

Chapter 29 — Mixed up Stories

Besides the occasional banging on the basement door it was very quiet until some of the kids got their stories all mixed up. They thought he was a bad German. They told their parents my Mom was hiding some Germans in our basement. One of them was very mean and would really hurt anyone who tried to get in there!

One morning to everyone's surprise, three policemen pounded on our front door. They forced their way past Mom and went into the kitchen. They ordered her to open the door leading down to our basement. She explained she couldn't because it was locked from the inside and she never had a key. One of the policemen muttered, "Likely story!" They all three pulled their guns from their holsters. Because of this commotion someone in the basement pounded on the door as loud as he could! Finally, one of the policemen broke the door down. Mom, firmly and quietly, told me to go into the living room and sit! I did! When I was much older, I heard the whole story from listening to the Ruark family members tell about the time those "Germans" hid in Mom's basement.

I learned those people in the basement were not really F.B.I. agents at all. They had been operating a bookie joint in Mom's basement. This meant Uncle Charlie's friends had been taking bets on the horse races over those phones and this was totally against the law. The mean German Shepherd belonged to one of the men who took the bets over the phone. Sometimes they would wrestle with the dog and that's when the kids heard the loud banging sounds on the basement door.

There were a lot of patriotic signs posted around in those times with a picture of a man named Uncle Sam. These were there to remind people of things they needed to remember during war times. One of the signs was Uncle Sam pointing his finger and the words under the picture said, "I want you!" This hopefully would encourage men to enlist. I remember another sign which read "Loose Lips Sink Ships!" I wondered what that sign meant.

MaMa remembered that sign and was quick to tell me, "It meant we should not talk about the war and spread false rumors. Those kids made up their stupid story just to cause trouble." She pantomimed a swat with her open hand as she said, "They were not raised high enough, hard enough, or often enough to learn to mind their own business and keep their mouths shut!"

Chapter 30 — Did She Know

Uncle Charlie didn't visit us for a while, but he got Mom a real good lawyer who never mentioned the name of Charlie Bartoleane. He convinced the judge Mom believed the men were F.B.I. agents who wanted to use her basement as a home base in Wilmington in an effort to track down war spies. He also explained the basement door opened out into the alley and those men had the only key. The door to the kitchen was locked from the inside. Since Mom never went into the basement, she did not get into trouble this time.

As usual Uncle Fred had to get in the last word when this story was told in the Ruark home. He'd look at Mom with his wicked grin and a Ruark twinkle in his eyes. Then he'd laugh loudly and wink at her. "Now, that's good for a laugh, Janey! But with your Ruark blood and brains I can't believe you'd fall for Charlie Boy's story. Admit it! You knew they weren't F.B.I. agents!" I wondered, *"Did Mom really know?"*

She didn't think this story was very funny. But the Ruark family loved it. They retold it every chance they got!

Chapter 31 — Silk Drawers

Uncle Charlie began visiting again after Mom's trial. One night when he was at our house Mom got a phone call from Aunt Edna who told her their Ma had a serious heart attack and was in the hospital. Aunt Edna was crying and told Mom she should come home right away. Mom did not have a car then and there were no trains or buses at such a late hour. She was in tears and so upset she just sat down and cried. Uncle Charlie took charge and insisted Tony could drive the three of us down to Salisbury. He woke me up, gathered my clothes and put me in his car with Mom after she grabbed her house keys and coat. Tony took off really fast! We screeched up to a sudden stop at the little hospital in Salisbury. The nurse in the admitting office told Mom Mrs. Ruark had been released. Back to the car, Mom gave Tony directions to Aunt Edna's, and we were off again. The worried Ruark clan was there gathered around MaMa's bed.

After things had settled down a bit Aunt Edna brought out some strong coffee and delicious cake for everyone. Mom finally had the chance to introduce Uncle Charlie. MaMa just kinda cleared her throat and gave Mom a hard look. Then she leaned over and whispered to Aunt Edna, "I told you so!" Of course, Uncle Fred had to start something. He began, "Wow, Mr. Bartoleane, that's sure a nice suit you're wearing. It looks like real silk! Is it?" Uncle Charlie proudly answered, "Yes, it is! My shirts and suits are all made by my tailor who has the cloth imported from China because they have the most exquisite silk materials. My tailor cuts and custom fits all of my clothes just my size." Uncle Elmer had listened to their conversation and shouted, "It must have taken a whole lot of material to make a suit big enough for a man as fat as you,

Charlie Boy!" All of the Ruark men burst out in loud laughter. Uncle Fred couldn't pass up his next comment. Grinning at Mom he shouted, "I'll bet his underdrawers are silk too!" Uncle Charlie jumped up and aimed a punch at Uncle Fred. He just ducked and gave Uncle Charlie an insulting pat on the face. Then Uncle Fred danced away across the room and stopped at the door. He sang out a little chant he made up:

"Uncle Charlie wears a silk shirt,
a silk suit and silk drawers, I'll bet!
He can't catch me! He's afraid to get wet!"

Then he raced out into the rain. PaPa hollered "Fred, watch out for Edna's cesspool!" His other three sons joined in the chase. Uncle Charlie took out after Uncle Fred into the dark night just like a hound dog after a coon! PaPa shouted, "They're heading out for the cesspool!"

That wicked rascal, Uncle Fred, jumped right over the cesspool! He stood there waving his arms to get Uncle Charlie to keep running after him. Poor Uncle Charlie was a city boy. He didn't even know what a cesspool was until he fell right into it! Phew! What a horrid smell!

PaPa's boys just stood around howling at the sight of poor Uncle Charlie threshing around in that stinky mess. PaPa shouted to his sons, "Stop this nonsense now! You boys get this poor man out of there this second!" His boys still couldn't stop their giggling as they made a feeble fumbling attempt to get Uncle Charlie out. PaPa made them pull off his messy clothes and even his nasty shoes and socks.

Aunt Edna ran out of the house with some towels and a couple of quilts to wrap around him. She kept apologizing for her brother's terrible prank. But Uncle Charlie didn't want to hear it. He just kept cussing and calling them things like ignorant hillbillys and uncivilized savages. I didn't know what he meant but I remembered it any way. Uncle Fred had to get the last laugh by holding up Uncle Charlie's wet underpants and calling out to Mom, "I told you so, Lady Janey! Silk drawers!"

Mom was horrified! She grabbed me and jumped into Uncle Charlie's car. Tony drove the three of us to Wilmington in complete silence with all the windows down to let in some fresh air. But the smell was still awful! I gagged and almost vomited.

We got back to Wilmington a lot quicker than we had got to Salisbury. No one spoke a word. I was quickly put to bed. I heard Uncle Charlie taking a shower. Tony mysteriously produced a fresh change of clothes for him. Then he drove Uncle Charlie off into the night in his long black car.

About a month later Aunt Edna brought MaMa up to Wilmington for a visit with us. When she asked about Mr. Bartoleane Mom just said, "My brothers ruined anything I was planning with Charlie. He would have been a good husband for me and a good father for Violetta."

MaMa just had to have the last word. She really loved her daughter and did not want her hurting about anything. She tried to speak in a gentler tone, "Now Janey, you know he wasn't the right man for you. He would never marry you. He's got other obligations. You don't want an uncle for Violetta. You need a father for her! You don't want her to be like Miss Brown's poor daughter, Betty Sue, with a whole string of uncles!"

Mom almost shouted, "I don't want to hear about this ever again!" She left the room and slammed the door as hard as she could.

Unfortunately, or fortunately, I'm not sure which, we never had any more visits from Uncle Charlie.

Chapter 32 — Sore Loser

Aunt Katherin told me this Ruark story. She said it happened about a month after the cesspool incident. Early in the morning before the sun came up a car drove up their lane and screeched to a stop. She heard a loud thud and the car took off. Slowly she opened the front door and saw a long black car speeding down their lane. She was surprised to see her husband, my Uncle Fred, crumpled in a heap on their porch. She managed to drag him into the living room. He was in pretty bad shape with blood all over his clothes.

"God almighty, Fred!" she cried, "What happened?" He could only moan before he passed out. She covered him with a quilt and sat by his side until the sun had risen. After he came to, she managed to wash most of the blood away and get him to their bed. She got him out of his nasty clothes and continued to sit by his side.

This time he was able to half explain he had been beaten up by a man who was just a sore loser in a card game. Uncle Fred said he had won a large sum of money fair and square. The man claimed he had won by dealing from the bottom of the deck. Uncle Fred also said the man and his two friends beat him up,

Sarah (MaMa), Lee (PaPa), Johnny, and Fred

took back the money he had honestly won, and dumped him on the porch. Aunt Katherin and everyone in the Ruark family believed his story. His brothers and even PaPa were all ready to go hunt those men down. Uncle Fred begged them not to because they had threatened to hurt his family if he told the sheriff or came looking for them.

Uncle Fred became a different kind of man. He stopped playing his tricks on anyone. He was strangely quiet for many years. His family was beginning to worry about him acting so strange and so quiet whenever he and Aunt Katherin came to the family's dinners.

Chapter 33 — Shopping for Shoes

Things were going smoothly for Mom and me in Wilmington. It was Sunday afternoon. She and I were walking up town. I noticed everyone on the street had long worried faces. There were no smiles anywhere. I asked her the reason for this. Mom tried very patiently to explain the difference between optimism and pessimism "Well, I guess it's because of this war in Europe. A lot of people here in America are worried. They are afraid we might still get involved."

I just wasn't getting it. "What does that have to do with shopping?" Her reply was, "Don't you remember like my Pa used to say, "It's always darkest before the dawn!" I persisted, "What do you mean?" We stopped and looked at some pretty shoes in the window of the Royal Shoe Store.

Mom smiled broadly and answered my question, "It means we should all stop worrying about this war in Europe so much. It means we both need a new pair of shoes!" She loved shoes more than she loved to eat. All the stores were closed on Sunday because of the Blue Laws. So, we went shoe shopping the next day after school and a very nice man, Mr. Neumann, waited on us. He helped Mom decide which shoes she wanted. He was a good salesman because she didn't buy the shoes she originally liked. He talked her into buying a whole different style. I heard her tell him he had a tongue as smooth as her fathers. I was too young to understand why she would tell him such a thing. But like my MaMa's wise old owl I was a good listener!

She explained to Mr. Neumann how people down home used to say her father was the most persuasive man around. His friends often said he had the smoothest tongue on the Shore.

He laughed and said, "What a funny thing to say!"

Mom continued and gave him a compliment often heard down home in Salisbury. She said, "Well, I think you've got my father beat. I'll bet you could sell a refrigerator to an Eskimo." They both had a good laugh.

It was good to hear two grownups laugh! I finally understood what Mom had been trying to tell me. "There's no reason to worry about things out of your control!" My MaMa once told me, "Worrying is like a rocking chair. It never takes you anywhere. It just gives you something to do!"

And sometimes PaPa would add with a smile, "Yep and worrying will give you wrinkles too!"

Chapter 34 — A Long Dinner

Mr. Neumann and Mom talked for a pretty long time. One of his employees told him it was closing time. He said to Mom, "We've talked so long, and your little girl has been so patient and well-mannered I'd really like to take you both out to dinner. Would you wait for a few minutes until I get the registers checked out?" To my surprise, Mom agreed. We went to a real fancy restaurant and had a wonderful dinner.

After our meal Mom reminded Mr. Neumann, he forgot to ask us for the ration stamps for her shoes. During the war everyone was issued a ration stamp when they needed to buy shoes. She looked in her purse and discovered she didn't have them with her. She promised she would bring them to him the next day. They both smiled a lot and seemed to enjoy dinner as much as I did. The banana splits he ordered for us finished off a perfect day for me even though Mom had forgot to buy my new shoes.

Chapter 35 — Tap Tap Tapping

It was almost closing time the next day when Mom took me back to the store to give Mr. Neumann the stamps she forgot to give him for her shoes.

Then her face turned a little red when she explained she forgot to buy my pair of shoes. I'll never forget the most beautiful shiny black shoes Mr. Neumann picked out for me. They had taps on the bottoms. They clicked when I walked, and I could even make them sound like I was tap dancing. I just loved them!

Violetta in tap shoes circa 1943

When Mom started to pay for my new shoes he laughed and said, "Oh no! I can't charge you for these. They are a late birthday or an early Christmas present from me!"

"Well," Mom asked. "Does this mean you'll be paying for dance lessons next?"

He was such a happy man. He laughed again and said, "Sounds like a good idea to me!" He smiled and winked at me. "How would you feel about trying some dance lessons?"

"Oh yes!" I almost shouted. I couldn't hear my tap shoes then as I skipped and hopped. I was floating on air!

Chapter 36 — Getting to Know You

The next day the workers at the shoe store teased Mr. Neumann. They asked him in a joking way how were they to decide which customer they should take out to dinner. One of them said, "You'll know it's getting serious if he asks her out for lunch and doesn't come back until the next afternoon!"

There was a lot of gentle laughter and knowing smiles when Mom came in with me at lunch time. Mr. Neumann gave them a little warning look and he turned a little red in the face. She gave him the ration stamp for her shoes and mine too. When we were leaving, he said softly to her, "I'll get off tomorrow at one o'clock. Come by and have lunch with me and we can continue our talk then."

He didn't have to go back to work until the next day. So, we had a very long lunch. Mom and Mr. Neumann talked and talked and learned a lot about each other. Of course, it was interesting, and I listened and listened! She shared the good things about her family. She just skipped over the part about Ralph's car, the crowbar and Uncle Charlie. She did tell him about some of the good things which happened to us since we came to Wilmington. He was delighted with her stories about Mom Toso and her son, Maurice.

Mr. Neuman explained, "My family were Jews and that crazy man, Hitler, had been trying to kill all of the Jewish people in Germany and Italy. My father had been killed by the German Gestapo. But my uncle had been able to get me, my sister, and my mother out of our country and come to America."

Mom asked him the name of his country in Europe where he had lived. He said they had lived in Hungry. I thought to myself, *"That must be the reason why he's so skinny!"*

I silently remembered, *"Uncle Johnny, Uncle Roy, and PaPa were all thin as a rail. People used to laugh and say, "Well, those three were so thin they'd each have to stand twice to make their own shadow." MaMa and Uncle Elmer were both short and round. Folks used to joke about the difference in their builds. They'd say Uncle Elmer was MaMa's favorite and she'd always put extra food on his plate. And they also said MaMa liked to taste everything two or three times while she was cooking."*

Mr. Neumann told Mom he had tried to enlist in the army because he was concerned our country, America, could be in danger if that crazy German, Hitler, decided to attack us here. But when he went to enlist his recruiting officer said he would have to be classified as a 4F because he was flat footed. He explained it was no disgrace but with all the marching required Mr. Neumann would not be able to stand the pain. Instead he was recruited as an Air Raid Warden. England was being heavily bombed from German airplanes at night. When the Wilmington air raid signal blasted out all the streetlights would shut down. Everyone had their windows covered with heavy dark drapes, so no lights could be seen. Mr. Neumann explained his job was to patrol the area where he lived and make sure there were no lights showing from the houses. This would prevent any enemies flying overhead from seeing where to drop their bombs.

He also told Mom his regular job was as a trouble shooter for the chain of Royal Shoe Stores. The big bosses sent him to a store where their business was showing a drop in sales. His job was to show the store manager and employees how to increase their business again. He explained the many different ways to do this. It could be done by something as simple as changing the lights and displays inside the store. Maybe it was because the manager wasn't ordering the latest styles wanted by their customers. Perhaps it was boring window displays. Last but certainly not least were the salespeople's interactions with the prospective customers. If that was the cause he would have to provide training for the employees. He was expected to solve whatever was causing the store's drop in business within the first year. The second year he was to observe and send reports along with their cash receipts to the corporate office. Once the store was showing a profit he would be sent to a different location. He explained he was transferred around a lot.

Janey (Mom) in Wilmington with school in background

Going out with Mr. Neumann got to be a habit. I believe Mom liked him as much as I did. One time he took us to a place called Horne and Hardart. He gave me a bunch of quarters and showed me how to select any food I wanted. I would put a quarter in the slot on the machine and a little window opened. I reached in and helped myself. This was the most fun. I liked Mr. Neumann a whole lot. Unlike Uncle Charlie he seemed to really like me too. He really knew how to have a good time. The best thing was he made Mom laugh a lot. I think that's why I liked him so much.

Chapter 37 — Adventures in Wilmington

We saw a lot of Mr. Neumann. He took us to the movies, the museum, and the zoo. We went to an aquarium and he even took us to see a real circus.

One Saturday when Mom had to work, he volunteered to take care of me. First, we rode on a streetcar which had a large sign, "Downtown Wilmington." It was a long ride and he told me all about streetcars. He knew a lot of things like when they were invented and what made them run. He told me some people called them trolleys. It was very interesting. We stayed on the trolley until we came to a big building with a large flashing sign, "Bowling Alley". He explained he played on a league there. I didn't understand exactly what he meant.

When we first went in it was very noisy. He shouted so loud it scared me half to death. I had never heard him shout before. "Quiet! Quiet! I've got my little girl with me today and there will be no profanity until after we leave!" I wasn't sure what the big word profanity meant. It must have been another word for noise because after he shouted it got almost as quiet as the Catholic school and church I went to. The big balls being thrown by some of the men made a terrible loud sound. It was so smoky in the room it made my eyes sting at first. I didn't see any women or little girls like me there.

But all of Mr. Neumann's friends treated me awfully nice. They bought me a candy bar, a comic book, two sodas, and a bag of peanuts! It was fun to watch him throw his big bowling ball and try to knock down those things he called pins. I couldn't even lift the ball. It was just too heavy. Before we left he explained his team had won. It was all very exciting and he was very happy about winning.

After getting back on the trolley we rode back up town

to the biggest library in Wilmington. He wanted to return some books he had borrowed. I didn't know you could borrow books. I thought you always had to buy them. Mom said we didn't have money to throw away on books we would never have time to read. She didn't know it but I used to read my comic books under my covers with a flashlight at night.

He told the library lady I wanted to get a book or two. She said either my mother or my father would have to sign a card for me first. "No problem.", he smiled as he signed for my card. I didn't tell the lady he wasn't my father. He signed me up like he was my real father and got me a library card of my own. He explained how it worked and told me not to lose it. After this he took me back to the library every Saturday morning. We returned the books from the week before and then checked out two new ones. He loved books and he loved to read. He bet me I could never in my life read all those books. I loved to read, and I said, "Maybe not. But I'd sure like to try!"

The best thing was it didn't cost us a dime, so Mom wouldn't be able to fuss about it. She did tell him he was going to spoil me and run out of things to make me happy. I was so glad we went shopping for shoes and met him.

Chapter 38 — Adventure in Pittsburgh

I had just come back to Wilmington after a visit with Aunt Edna. Norman was home in Salisbury waiting to start school again. Mom helped me get dressed as she explained we were going to take a short trip with Mr. Neumann. I had on my very best dressy dress and a cute little hat which was in style for young ladies. It had been copied from the hat soldiers wore during the war. It was much fancier though. It was trimmed with some lace and a tiny American flag sewed on the side of it. I also wore my new white crocheted lace gloves. Mom wore a skirt, a pretty white blouse, her wide brimmed hat, and her white silk gloves. She explained ladies always wore a hat and gloves when they were traveling. I was so excited! Mr. Neumann was going to show us where he was going to move and get another shoe store out of trouble.

Janey (Mom), Violetta, and Paul (Dad)

The name of the place was Pittsburgh Pennsylvania. I remember everything was very dirty and covered with really black dust. We went into the shoe store Mr. Neumann was supposed to fix the next time he got transferred. I leaned up to the counter while the grownups were talking. Oh, my goodness! When we were ready to leave, I had a giant black smudge across the whole front of my new dress. Mom and Mr. Neumann were not actually having an argument. They were talking rather crossly and impatiently though. She was fussing about the large black dots on her new white blouse and the nasty mark across the front of my dress. I wondered what this mess was. Mr. Neumann explained it was something called soot which came from the coal mines. "Well, I can see right now I have no intention of ever living here for any reason! Come on baby. Let's go home!"

And so we did. We didn't even get to eat in a restaurant there. The trip back to Wilmington was terribly silent. Both grownups didn't say a word. I just kept my eyes on the comic book Mr. Neumann had bought me. But it had a lot of nasty soot all over it. I didn't want to get my dress any dirtier, so I didn't even open it.

Chapter 39 — Traveling Alone

Saint Peter's school was closed for our summer vacation. Mom had promised me I could spend this time with MaMa on the Shore until September. Then I would have to go back to school in Wilmington again.

Mom let me talk with MaMa on the phone. She told me she really wanted me to visit with her for the whole summer. I shouted "Yah Whooo!" just like my PaPa did when he was excited and happy.

Violetta picking peaches on the Shore

My vacation began with me going back to the Shore on the Greyhound all by myself. Mom put me on the seat right behind the bus driver. He promised her no one would sit in the seat beside me and no one would bother me. He was a very nice man. When the bus had to make a rest stop he stood right outside the bathroom door and waited for me. He bought me a sandwich and a big bottle of real cold Coca Cola. Then back on the bus again. I enjoyed reading the comic book he bought for me at the rest stop. He told me he had a little girl about my age and she loved comic books. When the Greyhound pulled into the bus station in Salisbury Aunt Edna and MaMa were waiting for me. The bus driver got my suitcase out of the baggage compartment and put it in Aunt Edna's car.

They thanked the driver for watching out for me. I had finished reading my comic book so I gave it to the bus driver and asked him to give it to his little girl. We hopped in Aunt Edna's car and we were on our way to a glorious summer with my MaMa! "Yah Whooo!"

Chapter 40 — Told You So

MaMa called Mom on the telephone and told her I had arrived safely and not to worry about me. She would take good care of me and she did.

Mom called us about a week later. I thought she just wanted to check and see if I was happy. Of course, I was! I was with my MaMa! Mom told us she had got a job with the Lerner's Dress Shop. She liked the work and was making good money. She said the boarders were all still there and they had asked about me. I asked her about Mr. Neumann. She said he had been very busy and had not been around. That news was the only dark cloud over my vacation. I really liked him, and I thought he liked us too.

Aunt Edna was a lot like me. She had real sharp ears like a fox and she never missed much. When we finished talking on the phone she began asking me about Mr. Neumann. I filled her in and told her about all the fun things we had done and also about the nasty old Pittsburgh place. She and MaMa looked at each other in a strange way and just shook their heads. MaMa said to Aunt Edna, "I told you so!"

Janey (Mom), Nina, (Aunt Edna's daughter), and Aunt Edna

Chapter 41 — A Lot of Changes

My summer vacation was over. School in Wilmington would soon be starting. Mom came down to the Shore to take me back to our house on West Seventh Street in Wilmington.

There had been a lot of changes since I left. Mom's four roomers had now grown to be six boarders. This meant now she had to add enough potatoes and dumplings in the pot to feed six hard working men. Of course, it meant too, she would have more money on the table when they all finished eating.

She had a job at the Lerner's Dress Shop up town. She told me they paid her good and she also got a discount. She could buy her clothes cheaper there than any place else. She still bought her shoes at the Royal Shoe Store.

She saved the best news for last. Showing me a pretty ring on her left hand she explained, "Remember when your Aunt Edna and Nina came up to Wilmington to visit me for a little while when you were visiting with your MaMa?" Yes, I remembered. Mom had asked me to come too. But I didn't go because I wanted to stay with MaMa for the whole summer. Mom continued, "Well, when Edna came up here Mr. Neumann and I got married."

The best news of all was she had married Mr. Neumann! "He will be living with us now if you don't mind." She said, "You can call him dad if you don't mind."

Why would I mind? "Yah Whooo!" I was so happy! At last I had my very own real Dad! He was the best Dad anyone could ever wish for!

Chapter 42 — A Real Jewish Wedding

MaMa could hardly wait for Aunt Edna to return to Salisbury and tell her about Janey and Paul's wedding in Wilmington. Aunt Edna began, "Well, Ma, I've never seen anything like it in my whole life. It lasted for a whole day and half of that night. It seemed like all of Wilmington began arriving early that morning. They had brought a lot of food with them. They stayed for a while hugging and kissing and talking. Paul introduced each one of them to me. I could not understand a word they were saying. Paul had warned Janey and me to just hug them back and smile a lot.

Janey saw a group of young women standing close by. When she heard them giggling and saying the word "shiksa" a lot, she asked Paul what they meant. He just hugged her and said, "They are just saying how pretty you are." That made Janey so happy, she raised her arms high over her head and rushed over to them. Her intention was to say, thank you and give them a big hug!

They misunderstood and quickly scattered off like a flock of frightened quail. I don't think Janey ever found out they hadn't been saying she was pretty. They were actually joking because Paul was marrying a shiksa which meant someone who was non-Jewish!

Chapter 43 — Wedding Celebration

MaMa held her sides laughing loudly, and said, "If Janey ever finds that out I'm not sure if she will laugh or get mad. But tell me more about their wedding."

Of course, I listened intently and Aunt Edna continued, "Well, there were many more guests who arrived during the day bringing in food to be shared. Some of their guests also brought musical instruments. I thought it was strange though only the men danced. The women just clapped their hands and swayed to the music. Each of the male guests was expected to dance a short dance with the bride. It was customary for the bride to have a purse over her shoulder. Each of her dance partners were to put a sum of money into it. Paul told me this was to pay for the honeymoon. The last part of the wedding was when Paul and Janey stood under a white cloth canopy. They both stomped on a glass and broke it together. The guests cheered loudly and returned to their homes.

Left: Janey and Paul's sister
Right: Sarah Martha and Paul's mother

Chapter 44 – Eastern Shore Wedding

MaMa really enjoyed Aunt Edna's story. This led her to reminiscing about weddings in Salisbury. She began, "Weddings have sure changed here since my mother was married. In those times a preacher only came to Salisbury about once a year. But a couple would be married if they had at least four witnesses who could testify they had jumped over a broom together. Then when the preacher came to town, he would perform an actual wedding.

Sometime someone might play a trick or two on the happy couple. I remember once some rascally friends sawed the legs off their bed halfway through. Then they put an open jar full of bees on the floor under the bed. The plan was for the happy couple to undress, sit on the bed. They did and the bed fell and broke the jar which released the bees to swarm everywhere. It was pitch dark and the bride and groom tried to fight off the bees and find the door. When they opened it half the town was there laughing and applauding! After someone covered the bride and groom with a quilt, the spectators still laughing returned to their homes."

They both had a good laugh when Aunt Edna added, "Today, we just go to our church or courthouse to get married. An official asks if we promise to love, honor and obey. After an affirmative, yes, he announces, 'I now pronounce you man and wife.' And it only takes about fifteen minutes!"

Chapter 45 — Shirley Temple's Lesson

I remember one day very clearly when Aunt Edna came to visit us in Wilmington. She really enjoyed what she called window shopping. This was when you just went to look at all the pretty things in the stores. Then you came home with no packages. We left Mom at home to rest. She didn't see any sense window shopping and wishing for something she couldn't buy. She would much rather go real shopping.

I had learned I should be very well behaved and never fuss if I wanted to get a little toy. Then Aunt Edna would often get me one small toy or maybe a book or a puzzle. I knew how to read the price tags. I knew which price meant it was possible for me to get something which wasn't too expensive. If the tag only had two numbers, I would linger a while and look at it wistfully. It always worked! This time she bought a bright red yo-yo for me because I was so well behaved. She only paid ten cents for the yo-yo.

As we were walking out of the store, I saw the most beautiful doll in the world. Aunt Edna told me about the movie star named Shirley Temple. She wanted to do something to help raise money to help in the war. So, she gave permission for people who made dolls to make a doll which looked just like her. When it was bought a large part of money it sold for went into the war effort in Europe. She wanted her doll to be dressed like the nurses who were in this war. So, the doll wore a doll sized white nurse uniform. There was a large Red Cross patch sewed on the bib of her white apron. She also had a beautiful blue cape just like the real nurses. On top of her curly hair she had a small white nurse's cap. I had to stop and point out every detail to Aunt Edna. She agreed with me the doll was beautiful. She reminded me this was only a window-shopping trip. She said she didn't have enough money to buy such a gorgeous doll. "Maybe Santa Claus will bring it to you this Christmas," she said.

"Who was she kidding?" I thought, *"Christmas was a long time away and I knew some lucky girl would have her mom or dad buy it for her today or tomorrow."* I wanted to fuss but I knew a tantrum wouldn't work. I remembered vividly how Aunt Edna had cured Norman of having his temper fits. And if I did make a scene, she would most likely never take me window shopping ever again.

When we got to my house I rushed in breathlessly and told Mom all about the beautiful doll. I pleaded, "Oh Mom! Please say I can have her! She will make me so happy and I promise I won't ask for another toy for a whole year!"

She very quietly asked me, "Is it your birthday?"

"No," I smiled, "You know it's not my birthday!"

"Well then your answer is no!" she said. After a pause she calmly asked. "Is it Christmas?"

"Don't be silly!" I laughed. "No. You know it's not Christmas."

Mom continued quietly and firmly, "Then again your answer is No! You know our present getting days have always been for birthdays or Christmas." She walked into the kitchen to finish fixing dinner. I sulked and moped around the house the rest of the afternoon.

When Dad came in from work, I gave him a big hug and kiss with my biggest smile. I quickly climbed onto his lap and told him all about the beautiful nurse doll.

I ended by asking if he would get her for me and I told him I would be the happiest girl in the world. Before he could answer I gave him another big hug and kiss and said, "I love you so much and I'm so glad you are my Dad. You are the best

Dad in the whole wide world."

Mom called in from the kitchen, "O.K. you guys it's time for your dinner."

The next night I was sitting on the front steps. When I saw Dad coming down the street from work, I ran to meet him. Sure enough, he had a large box under his arm. "I believe this is for my favorite daughter," he laughed.

I knew I was his only daughter. I tore open the box and there she was! I danced around him happily and gave him another big hug and kiss. "Oh, thank you Daddy! You are really the best Dad in the whole world!"

My biggest mistake was when I gave Mom a smirky little smile. She just let it go and made no comment about my new doll. When I came home from school the next day, I couldn't find my doll anywhere. I was smart enough to know I had best not ask Mom where she was. I wondered if she had thrown her in the garbage or maybe the store took her back.

When we finished supper, we went into our living room. Mom brought my doll in and said, "This is a very beautiful doll and she really should have a place of honor in our home. I've decided to put her up here on our mantle so she can remind us of the war. She will remind us how lucky we're not living in those countries where people are not as blessed as we Americans are."

Maybe! But my Shirley Temple doll didn't ever remind me of the war or any unfortunate people. She always reminded me Mom's word was the law!

After my nurse doll episode, it was very strange my little schemes never seemed to work. Whenever I asked Dad for something he would always say, "What does your mother think? We'd better ask her first."

The mystery was solved years later. At a Ruark family

gathering, I learned Mom and Dad would wait till I was asleep, take a walk around the block for a talk, and reach a decision they both agreed on.

Chapter 46 – My Hero

I couldn't always figure out Aunt Edna's youngest son, Norman. It seemed like he always enjoyed making me cry. When I'd decided I didn't really like him then he'd change quickly just like the chameleon we had studied about in school that could quickly change his colors. I remember once on his summer school break. It was his turn to visit us in Wilmington. He was trying to teach me to roller skate. Like his mother, Aunt Edna, he didn't have a lot of patience and when I fell, he'd fuss with me. Then he'd make me get up and try again and again! Anyway, we were together and outside playing. I was laughing, crying, and trying hard to learn how to skate. I thought he was an excellent skater! My knees were all scratched and bleeding from falling. I tried hard not to complain or fuss. I was just happy he was spending so much time with me. A big boy came walking up the sidewalk. He stuck out his foot and tripped me on purpose! I fell hard and it really hurt! I just sat there and cried as loud as I could.

I thought my crying had scared the mean boy because he started to run fast. Then I realized it wasn't my crying scaring him. It was Norman who was chasing him on his skates. His little fists were clenched tight and he looked furious. He intended to beat this big bully up if he could catch him. He gained on the boy and grabbed for his jacket. He caught it and threw it on the ground. The boy raced up the steps of St Peter's and ran inside. Norman knew he couldn't fight inside of the church. So, he just sat down by the door and waited. When I came limping up, he said, "He's got to come out sometime. When he does, I'm going to make him sorry he tripped you!" I was so proud of my hero! I sat down beside him. When it started getting dark and cold, I thought we should go home.

Norman wrapped the bully's coat around my shoulders to keep me warm. He was adamant! He wasn't leaving until bully boy came out. It was getting really dark now. I sat down beside him. When it started getting even darker, I thought we should go home. The longer Norman sat the madder he got. Finally, I gave up. It was getting really dark now. I knew we'd both be in big trouble if Mom got worried about us. Besides I was afraid of the dark ever since Norman had taken me to see a horror movie about a

St. Peter's Cathedral in 2019

mummy and a wolf man almost a year ago. I ran quickly home and told Mom what happened. She went and got Norman who was still sitting on the church steps. After giving him a loud lecture, she made him come home with her.

    I noticed after she calmed down and realized Norman had been my protector she gave him a big hug and a bigger bowl of ice cream! And I was glad! Years later when the family was talking about his brave deed someone asked Norman what he learned on the church steps. "Well", he laughed, "One thing I learned was churches have two doors just like houses! The bully boy ran like a scared rabbit! He was probably home before I got to the top of the steps. But I think I taught him a lesson too. From then on whenever he saw us playing on the sidewalk he'd cross over the street and continue his walk on the other side!"

Chapter 47 — A Lesson to Remember

Another funny thing happened to Norman and me on one of his visits in Wilmington. Mom had put us to bed for the night. Neither of us could remember the reason why but we got a terrible case of the giggles and could not stop. Finally, Mom shouted for us to stop but we didn't. She put up with it for a while. Finally, her Ruark impatience gave way and she burst into our bedroom. She threatened us firmly we had better stop and go to sleep. We honestly tried but it was hopeless. The giggles kept coming! They just wouldn't stop. I can't remember who got the bright idea. I think it was Norman because he was the older one. Anyway, we continued with the giggling.

"I've warned you two for the last time!" Mom shouted as she charged into the room.

Wow! Was she mad!

She yelled loudly, "I'm going to whup, spank, and beat you til you learn I mean business!" She continued, almost screaming "I'll give you a lesson you won't forget!" Still yelling she pulled back the covers to discover we had put our pillows in the bed and covered them up with our quilts. She had really beat the feathers right out of those pillows! We were hiding safely in a corner of the room and again burst out giggling.

Mom grabbed Norman by his ear and me by the hair of my head. Still yelling she threw each one of us into a separate corner of the room. "Now," she screamed, "Stay there 'til I tell you to come out!" She stormed out and slammed the door.

We didn't giggle any more. It was hard not to because she had looked so silly whipping those pillows. We waited for her to come back and say we could get out of the corner. She didn't come back until the sun was peeking out. When she came into my room, she saw two pitiful little children still slumped in our corners. We were both sound asleep. We were too afraid to come out of the corner and get in bed. We had obeyed her final command. She was right, too. She gave us a lesson we have both remembered for a long, long time.

Chapter 48 — Please God

I was in Wilmington with Mom and my Dad. Supper was over. All of Mom's boarders were welcome to sit in our living room with us just like one big family. This was our time to relax with a good book, listen to the radio or maybe play a game of checkers. Dad didn't have to do his wartime job of Air Raid Warden tonight because the air raid alarm had been silent.

Suddenly there was a loud bang which came from the basement. Everyone jumped! We were all still on edge worrying about those crazy Germans. Maybe their planes had crossed the Atlantic Ocean after all. Mom spoke calmly, "Not to worry!" she said. "It's probably just a garbage can being blown around by the wind."

It had snowed, and a chilly wind was blowing around the house. It was kind of a spooky sound now and making a weird whistling noise. The windows were rattling like someone or something was trying to get in. But we were all warm and toasty. Mom said, "Like bugs in a rug."

Suddenly we heard a low rumbling sound coming from the basement. I usually believed what Mom told me but now I was still sure a bear must have crawled from the street into our basement.

Dad assured me there were no bears roaming the streets at night in Wilmington. I tried to believe him. But it growled again and was even louder! I was sure it was a huge bear with sharp claws and a very big mouth. The growling continued getting louder and louder. The radiators started banging and clanging. The bear was probably hitting those heat pipes with his big claws.

What a racket! I clapped my hands over my ears. But I

could still hear it. "Bang bang clank rumble arruh!" It was awful! BOOM!

I jumped into Mom's lap, held her tight, and closed my eyes. It sounded like someone tried to shoot the old bear! Just then Pop DelaRosa came running out of the bathroom with his pants down around his ankles! He was screaming loudly, "Missa Jeanie! Missa Jeanie! My ass'ah! My ass'ah! She's onna fire! She's onna fire!" He kept jumping up and down like an Indian doing a war dance.

Dad dashed down into the basement! *"Oh God,"* I prayed silently, *"Please don't let my Dad get killed by a bear or some Germans! Please God Please! He's the only Dad I've got. Please don't let him get killed!"* All the noise stopped. It was deathly quiet. Dad came back up the steps into the living room. He had a big smile on his face. "Everything's fine! I fixed it by turning off the fuse. We'll have to call a furnace repair man in the morning. We better all get to bed and wrap up for now."

Mom handed Pop DelaRosa a quilt from the couch. He wrapped it around his shoulders and headed to his room. The boarders went to their rooms. After a lot of giggling about Pop

Janey (Mom) Nina (Edna's eldest), Violetta, Pop DelaRosa, and Joanne (Nina's daughter)

DelaRosa's "assah" they finally settled down and went to sleep. Mom, Dad, and I went into our bedrooms and retired for the night.

The next day the repair man, Mr. Able, came and fixed the furnace. Then he, Dad, Mom, and I went downstairs to the basement. He explained the pipes were so old and filled with rust the water couldn't flow. It just kept heating like water does in a pot with a lid on tight. When the water got too hot it boiled up and exploded upstairs into the toilet where Pop DelaRosa had been sitting. Mr. Able assured us this would never happen again because he had replaced the bad pipes. We believed him, but no one was ever able to convince Pop DelaRosa.

After this when one of the roomers saw Pop DelaRosa heading for the bathroom he'd shout out "Look out! Here comes the Flash!" Pop DelaRosa came out of the bathroom as quickly as he went in. Someone would see him running to his room. Then with a big laugh a couple of the borders would shout, "There goes the Flash!" I didn't understand their joke until one day Mr. Conner bought me a comic book about the Flash. I learned the Flash was a superhero who moved faster than you could see him. That's what Pop DelaRosa was doing. He was trying to move as fast as the Flash so the hot water wouldn't come up and burn his assah again!

Chapter 49 — Never Ever Never

Summer vacation again and I was back with MaMa and Aunt Edna. She had made up her mind this was a good time to teach me how to keep a house spic and span just like her sister, Carey, had taught her. But I think her real reason was just to get me to keep her house so clean it would sparkle brightly for her company. Her idea of cleaning was to sit and read a magazine and tell me what to do. I remember one time, in particular, when she told me to sweep her kitchen floor because this was another one of those days when our preacher was to come for a visit. I didn't argue with her. I just got the broom and dustpan.

I guess I did protest a little when I said, "He doesn't even have to go into the kitchen."

She quickly replied, "If he goes out to use the outhouse he'll have to go outside through the kitchen!"

After I finished my chore I went in to get her to come and see the good job I thought I had done. When she finished reading her magazine she came into the kitchen.

To my surprise she just said, "Humph! If that's the best you can do, give me the broom and I'll do it myself." Guess what? She thought she was boss, but I never, ever, never swept a floor for her again!

Chapter 50 — Still Terrified

Aunt Edna was expecting our preacher to pay his weekly visit again. She told me to go in the kitchen and put some water in her new glass coffee pot and put it on the stove to heat. When the hot coffee was ready, I sat it down on the metal kitchen table. To my surprise as soon the hot coffee pot touched the cold metal it shattered to pieces! Aunt Edna rushed in to see what had happened. She gave me a hard smack to my head, threw me a tea towel, and told me in a low threatening tone to clean up the mess of broken glass.

Well, I'm almost eighty-six years old now and to this day I cannot cook anything in a pot or pan made out of glass. I'm still terrified it will shatter! Even though my grandchildren try to reassure me it really won't.

Chapter 51 — Money Maker

On a few of my visits with Norman and Aunt Edna, I had some good times! After Mr. Pottle disappeared Aunt Edna married a second man, Wayne Cloud. With a name like Cloud everyone thought he must have been an Indian. We didn't care or even notice his skin was a shade darker than ours. He was a very nice man. Norman now had a stepfather and I was to call him Uncle Wayne.

There were very few jobs on the Shore to be had so he developed his own business. He told us first you had to find out what was needed. Then you had to sit and think of how you could provide a way to fill that need. He became what was known as a traveling salesman. He'd buy various things he believed were necessary in someone's home. They might be such things as dishes, coffee pots, scrub boards, and whatever his customers requested. He bought his things at a low wholesale price and sold them at a high retail price. He'd load up his car and drive around Salisbury shouting like the fish man. But he never mentioned fish. He'd holler," Come See! Come Buy! Come Save!" Everyone would come rushing out of their houses and buy a lot. His secret salesman trick was he'd let them pay for those items with a small payment each week. He had a good business and made a lot of money. He always had money in his pocket and could buy anything he wanted. He was very fond of Norman and often bought him things Aunt Edna definitely wouldn't approve of.

When Norman was eleven and I was six Uncle Wayne gave him a small 22 rifle and a box of bullets. Norman was so excited. Trembling he grabbed Uncle Wayne and shouted," For Me? Really for me?"

Uncle Wayne just put his fingers to his lips and went out to his car to make some more money.

This present caused Norman to think and try to figure how he could make money like Uncle Wayne.

After some serious thinking Norman remembered how all those pesky rats at the city dump were a big problem. They were multiplying like mosquitoes and were beginning to expand their territory by wandering into town.

After telling me he had found the problem. I just said, "So, now what is your solution?" He patiently explained his solution to me.

His idea was to go down to the city dump and make an agreement with the owner. He said he would use his gun to shoot those pesky rats which lived there. He offered to charge only a quarter for each one he shot. Like his grandfather, Lee Bahnum Ruark, Norman was a good talker and a great shooter! The next day when Aunt Edna was taking her afternoon nap Norman and I slipped quietly out of the door and straight to the dump. He whistled for his little rat terrier and she came running. We three made a good team. Trixie dug those rats out of the holes they were hiding in. She barked loudly and scratched furiously. Norman shot and shot. He never missed one rat. I cheered them on! Norman shared his money with Trixie and me. He bought her some real good dog food. He and I had a lot of sodas, ice cream, and several movies that summer!

Chapter 52 — Grumble and Mumble

It took a while but eventually things got back to normal. It was summer, and school was out again. I was back at MaMa's and Aunt Edna's. It was Friday night and as usual I asked her if she'd take me swimming tomorrow. Then like Nancy used to say, "MaMa is going to start to grumble and mumble!" And her tirade always began, "Do you think I've got nothing to do except take you swimming? This ole house could use a good sweeping. I've got to get groceries, do some washing, then there's the ironing. This is the day the old fishman will come driving around in his wagon shouting, 'Fish for sale! Fish for sale! Get 'em while they're fresh!' I'm going to buy half a trout and one of those tasty rock fish. Like as not I'll have to gut and clean them myself. Lately he's getting' lazy like everyone else. He used to clean all the fish I bought. Now he says he doesn't have time. He's too busy. I guess he expects me to do his job. I reckon he is too busy going swimming."

Sarah Martha (MaMa)

Chapter 53 — Getting Ready

The next morning the rooster hadn't even crowed yet to wake us up. I heard MaMa yell from the hall downstairs. "Well, are you going to sleep the day away? I thought you wanted to go swimming!"

"Come get your breakfast before it gets cold!" I didn't need to be called twice. I jumped out of my nice warm bed onto her frigid bedroom floor. It was so cold I thought I could feel ice on the linoleum under my bare feet. I grabbed a quilt from the bed and wrapped it tight around me. Next, I flew down those freezing steps into her toasty warm kitchen full of delicious smells.

Sarah Martha (MaMa)

The table would be set complete with a beautiful white crocheted tablecloth she had made many years before. It looked as though she was expecting some company. There were no mismatched, cracked, or broken dishes ever on her table. She never threw anything away though. She always said, "You never know when you might need something." She stored those pieces out of reach on the highest shelves in Aunt Edna's kitchen cupboards as she used to say, "Just in case." And there they stayed. She believed in using her best things for her family. "Because", she explained, "my family is more special to me than any of my friends or neighbors. I like to use pretty things for my own pleasure too."

The food aroma inviting me to come quickly into the kitchen was just a hint of what was to come. After she said the blessing, we began with a glass of fresh squeezed orange juice. This was followed by some home-made biscuits she had just baked. We finished off the scrapple, eggs, and hot cakes with honey and butter. We also had a pitcher of fresh milk nice and cold from the icebox for me. MaMa had a pot of strong black coffee to enjoy. She didn't believe in children drinking coffee unless it was to chase the bad tasting cod liver oil medicine out of your mouth. Cod liver oil was a real nasty medicine you had to take if you were ever real droopy or if you got tired real easy. It tasted so awful! You can bet I never complained I was never even just a little bit tired!

We cleared the table and put the milk and orange juice in the ice box. There was no food to save. We had put everything away in our stomachs. To tell the truth I felt like I should go back upstairs, crawl under those quilts and take a nice long nap. I smiled contentedly at MaMa. She was sorta lingering over her coffee and I noticed she had her Sunday sunbonnet on to keep the sun from shining in her eyes. We were almost ready to go.

But first the dishes were put in the dish basin which I carried outside to the ole pump bench. I primed the pump and filled the dish basin about half full of cold water. MaMa followed me out with a tea kettle filled with boiling water she had heated on her stove. She poured this in with the cold water and washed the dishes. I rinsed them with the cold pump water and put them on a large tray she had brought out. She carried the clean dishes into the house and set them to dry on her countertop. She didn't believe in drying dishes with a tea towel, "Because," as she said, "that's how you get those nasty germs and get sick."

Now maybe we were really ready to go. She grabbed her big black purse and a large basket which I learned later had fried chicken and biscuits for our lunch. Hanging the basket over her arm she reminded me to get my swimsuit, towels, and wide brimmed hat. It was summer and it was getting warmer out side. She lowered the window shades to keep the afternoon sun out and keep the house cooler. I thought, *"Now we can go."* I noticed she never locked her doors when she went any place. I asked her why and she explained, "Locks only keep honest people out. You can't lock a house up tight enough to keep a crook out!"

"Yes," I thought silently, *"but I think I'll make it more difficult for the crook and lock my house when I'm grown."* I really didn't agree with her. But there was no sense starting a fuss about it. I had learned I couldn't win and besides it was too pretty a day to argue and I was actually ready to go swimming!

Chapter 54 — A Day in the Park

A really good memory I have about my vacations with MaMa was the walk from Short St. down to the City Park. There was a lovely stream of the Wicomico River flowing through the middle of the park. It was there I learned to swim. But it was also a long walk especially on a really hot day.

MaMa would say, "We'll just put one foot in front of the other one." We did while we sang some of her church songs. We got there without a single grumble.

I spread our towels out. One was for MaMa to sit on. The other was for me to dry off with after I went swimming. She started up again. "Now don't you start pestering me about getting any ice cream when the ice cream man drives around and rings his bell!"

"Oh MaMa, I promise I won't. I'll be so happy to be swimming I probably won't even hear him." Before she could

Violetta and Sarah Martha (MaMa)

add another "don't" I ran squealing and jumped into the cold water. The happiest days I spent in Salisbury were with my MaMa. Ah, Heaven! I swam until my fingers looked like little dried up raisins. I finally got tired and got out of the water and wrapped myself up in my towel. I was as warm as I could be. We devoured our lunch which she had spread out. Now I was ready to run and jump into the icy water and enjoy more swimming.

"No, you don't!" she yelled. "You have to wait for ten minutes before you go back into cold water!" I was in for another big lecture. "You might get a bad cramp and sink to the bottom and drown. Then I wouldn't have no little girl to love and keep my feet warm at night." I must confess I wasn't happy, but I obeyed and just sat at the edge of the shoreline with my feet dangling in the water. This was always the longest ten minutes I ever had to endure.

As I was sitting there I heard her shout my name. I thought she was going to tell me it was time to go home. She marched up to where I was and yelled at me so everyone there could hear. "Get yourself up here now!"

I was expecting to be thrashed though I couldn't guess why. I jumped up so fast I stumbled and fell.

"Can't you hear his bell? You better get these two nickels if you want to buy an ice cream cone for you and one for me. I know I want one to cool myself down. It sure is hotter here than the devil's own kitchen!"

Well now I couldn't and didn't argue with her. But I thought if she would have jumped in the water with me she would have been a lot cooler.

After we finished our ice cream MaMa got up from the towel she had been sitting on. She moved up to sit on a park bench. "This ground's as hard as a piece of cement," she complained.

"I need to rest my bones before we start back home." I never figured this out because the bench was really cement and the ground was just dirt.

Anyway, then she'd take out her bible and read an hour or two while I was swimming again. "All right," she'd abruptly announce. "We're done here. It's time to be getting home." She seemed happy on the way home. She frequently said, "The best part of leaving home is the coming back." I think about her saying that now whenever our family is returning home after going on a trip. She was a little breathless from climbing the hill back to Short Street. But she never stopped her chatter. "You have been so well behaved today I'm going to let you scale and gut our fish for supper when we get home."

"Wow!" I felt like a big grown up lady scaling and gutting those fish on the pump bench in her backyard. She trusted me with her big sharp knife only grownups were allowed to use. It was the end of a perfect day! I never could understand why Uncle Fred's daughter, Nancy, just couldn't tolerate her. She said it was because MaMa grumbled and mumbled so much. I had learned not to pay too much attention to her grumbling. I loved my MaMa! I still do! I know she loved me too!

Chapter 55 — Breath in my Body

One weekend Mom came down to the Shore when I was there on vacation with MaMa. Aunt Edna had called and told her Aunt Carey was terribly sick. When Mom arrived she took MaMa, Aunt Edna, and me to see for ourselves if Aunt Carey was as sick as everyone said. Most everyone thought she was probably going to die.

The rest of the Ruarks, were all gathered around her bed with her husband and children when we arrived. Her preacher was also there. Aunt Carey didn't do anything except lay in bed and complain. She said she would probably die of starvation because Uncle Tom didn't even know how to make her a decent cup of tea. MaMa offered to come "just for a short visit and try to help out a bit." Aunt Carey just kept getting weaker and weaker. Everyone in the family was really worried.

Uncle Tom just couldn't believe she was really sick. They had been married twenty years and she was normally healthy as a horse. He secretly told Mom his wife enjoyed being the family drama queen. He asked Mom if she would help with a little idea he had to get Aunt Carey back on her feet. Of course, I listened as they plotted what they were going to say for her to hear. It was kinda funny something like Uncle Fred might do.

We came back to visit the next day and Uncle Tom and Mom stood out in the hall near Aunt Carey's bedroom, so she could hear them. Mom, pretending to be worried about her said to him, "Well Tom, I don't know how much longer she can last." Then he said, "Yes, it's really sad to think about. I guess though I'll have to keep on going for my children. They're so young. They'll really need a mother to help me raise them." He paused and then added, "That reminds me, Janey. I was wondering if you could drive back down next week and sit with Carey for a day?" With a twinkle in his eyes and a wicked little grin he continued, "You know the pretty young widow who lives down the road. I've been thinking about her a lot lately. She really needs a man to help her with some of those hard jobs on her farm. I think I should go over to her place a couple days of the week and help her out." Mom answered in an excited voice, "Oh, Tom, that sounds like an excellent idea. I know she'd appreciate it and if you ever needed her to help you with the children, she'd be glad to return the favor."

It had been very quiet in Aunt Carey's room and then the three of us heard her say, "Humph!"

Later on, MaMa told us Aunt Carey got out of bed the next day very early in the morning. She got all dressed up and had Uncle Tom's breakfast on the table when he got up.

Once I overheard her saying to MaMa, "Little widow hussy down the road needn't get any ideas in her head she'll get my man, move into my house, and raise my children! No indeed! Not as long as I've got breath in my body she won't!"

There was never any more talk from Aunt Carey about being sick or dying.

Chapter 56 — Summer Retreat

One of the best things I remember about my summer vacations was the time MaMa and I rode on the church bus to the Carey's Camp Ground Retreat near Millsboro Delaware. We stayed for a whole week. It was like nothing I had ever seen before. There were these tiny little wood houses which were all built side by side. There was a row of these houses on each side of a big empty space called the promenade. Teenagers, young single people, and children would walk around in this big empty space. They would talk, giggle, and flirt under the watchful eyes of their parents and other church members sitting in their chairs lined up at the front of their houses.

These houses were not furnished and lacked any kind of modern facilities. You could bring some comforts of home like quilts, sheets, and pillows. Everyone brought one dish and one cup for each person in their cabin. You would also need a knife, fork, and spoon for each one. There was no such thing as paper or plastic plates in those days. You had to bring your own food too. It had to keep well and last you for a week. There was also an ice box to help keep your food from spoiling if you remembered to bring a quarter for the ice man. MaMa brought a frying pan, a stewing pot, and her coffee

Carey's Camp Marker in 2019

pot. Of course, you needed a dish basin to wash your dishes in. You got your water out of the pump in the back yard. Last but certainly not least there were two restrooms available. One was for women and the other was for the men. Just like today except they were both outside and way down at the end of two separate paths!

There was a group prayer every morning. Breakfast was fixed and eaten. When this was finished everyone went outside with their chairs and listened to the preacher give his sermon. He stood up on a tall wooden box and talked very loudly so everyone could hear him. This was always an exciting time with a lot of hand clapping accompanied with shouts of "Praise the Lord," "Amen," and "Halleluiah." I heard some

Carey's Camp in 2019 showing the Central Meeting Hall

people remarking this preacher was "One of those Hell-Fire and Brimstone preachers."

After the preaching it would be time for lunch which took about two hours. The promenade came after this and took a long time. The young folks would just wander about and chat especially with the opposite sex. Younger children wandered off and got busy with jumping rope, hopscotch, hide and seek, and other games. The old folks would sit out in front of their little houses and take this time to visit, read their bibles, and catch up on the latest news. At the same time, they would be closely watching the behavior of those on the promenade. Next everyone would retire inside their little houses to rest both their soul and their body with a long nap. This was followed by a great supper. Sometimes there would be some people who wanted to do some testifying. Then the hymn sing would follow. There was always a joyful noise made unto the Lord. I guess it was joyful because everyone had rested up and their bellies were all full. After the hymn sing the old folks would read their bibles, visit and catch up on the latest news. Nothing was left to do now but get a good night's sleep and wait until the morning when we'd do it all over again. It was a fun time and looked forward to by all the people there. This gathering provided them with the chance to meet new Christian families and socialize with them. People often lived far apart from their neighbors and did not have much contact. Most everyone saw these retreats as an opportunity to give praise to the Lord and to make arrangements to get their teenagers engaged to be married to a suitable Christian person.

(Happy Memories)

Chapter 57 — A Good Lawyer

Soon after this Mom, Dad, and I were again going to visit Aunt Edna down in Salisbury. Mom was taking a large bowl of homemade vegetable soup to help her a little with her large number of family house guests. Dad had held it in his lap all the way from Wilmington. I was on the back seat of the car. We were at the corner of Brown and Naylor Streets in Salisbury. Mom was supposed to go, and the other man should have stopped because there was a stop sign on his street. He drove his car through his stop sign and rammed into us. Mom's car was a well-built Hudson Terraplane. She called it a Terrible Pain. It was a good car with a steel reinforced frame and excellent brakes. The other man's car was a total wreck. Ours was a total mess inside. Mom's vegetable soup went everywhere! Front, back, and sideways! Dad grinned sheepishly and said, "It's true, sweetie, I love your home-made vegetable soup! But not in my hair!"

The new firehouse was on our side of the street. It was a nice Eastern Shore day. The firemen were all sitting outside, and they saw what happened. There was no such thing as cell phones then. One of the firemen ran inside and called the police right away. When they saw mom crying, they all rushed up to see if they could help. She was a tough calculating lady, but she always knew when to turn on her tears.

The man who caused the accident kept shouting, "It was her fault! She caused it! Stupid woman shouldn't be driving anyway!" The police officer responded quickly and wrote up Mom's account of the accident. He said Mom and the other man would have to appear in court and let the judge settle this case of who did what. Then he went to question the other driver.

Mom told Dad she wasn't too worried because several of the firemen had offered to go to court as her witnesses. They said they would testify in her favor. She continued in a whisper, *"There is however one catch and cause for worry. I've been driving without a driver's license!"* When Dad heard this, he was completely flustered and at a loss for words. He was finally able to stammer out, "How can that be?" The only excuse she had was she had been too busy!

Like all the Ruarks, Mom was a quick thinker. The police officer came back and asked what her name was. She smiled so sweetly and answered without hesitation, "Frances Ruark." I saw Dad sort of stagger and softly mutter, "Oh, my God!" You may remember Frances Ruark was Uncle Johnny's wife. Mom knew Aunt Frances had a driver's license. This was getting to be more interesting by the minute!

I knew what she was saying was not true. But I had also been taught I should never contradict anything she ever said, or I would get into a mess of trouble. I just silently thought to myself, *"Great Mom! Now how are you going to get out of this kettle of fish?"*

The officer asked for her registration card and driver's license. Talk about an actress! She put on a great show of being so upset and confused. I knew she didn't have a registration card and she knew she didn't even have a driver's license! However, she started looking in her purse frantically for something she never had. Then she acted as though she was about to faint and began trembling and crying. Like most men the police officer couldn't stand to see such a pretty woman break down in such a frantic display of helplessness. He told her he would let her rest a bit while he interviewed some of the firemen who said they had seen the whole accident. He was so sorry she had to go through all of this. He said he completely understood how

Salisbury Fire Company No. 2 in 1935 (l) and 1950 (r)
Pictures courtesy of the
Salisbury Fire Department Museum archives

upset she was. Actually, he didn't know or understand the half of it! When he finished with the firemen, he returned to my sobbing mother. He told Dad to take her home and perhaps call a doctor. I sure didn't understand when he said she really needed something for her nerves. She didn't need anything for her nerves! She had more nerve than anyone I ever knew! The police officer had forgotten all about needing to see her license or registration card. He helped Dad get her into the car on the passenger side. Then he held the other door open for Dad. He slid hurriedly in the seat on the driver's side and held tightly onto the steering wheel. I thought, *Oh great! I knew he didn't have a driver's license either! I wondered was it just our family or did all adults do crazy stuff like this?*

As soon as we got home Mom called Aunt Frances and Uncle Johnny. They came over and put their heads together and tried to figure out a plan to solve the next part of Mom's predicament. They hired a lawyer who was a good friend of their father. When everyone appeared in court the man who hit us began yelling. "She's the one!" He kept interrupting the judge who stood his outbursts as long as he was able. Finally, the judge banged his gavel and yelled at the man as loud as he could, "Sit down and shut up! This is my courtroom and I'll decide who is guilty!" The judge then heard a testimony from one of the firemen. Mom's lawyer asked if he might approach the judge's bench. After the lawyer apologized to the judge, he presented Mom's case as he knew it. Then he added, "Your honor, this fine upstanding young lady is the daughter of Lee Bahnum Ruark!"

"Why in tarnation didn't you say so in the first place? We could have saved a lot of time. The Ruarks and I go a long way back. I knew Lee and his boys quite well, but I wasn't aware he had such a fine young daughter. Case dismissed!" And Mom didn't even need to try and use Aunt Frances' driver's license!

It wasn't long before Salisbury had a four way stop sign at the intersection of Brown and Naylor streets. The story of Mom's stop sign was often a favorite memory to share at the Ruark's get-togethers. Ruark friends and family referred to the stop sign as a warning sign that Janey was back in town! And when this story was told PaPa laughed and said, "This just goes to show you how important it is to have friends, like lawyers and judges, in high places.

Chapter 58 — More about Life

I learned a lot of school stuff in Wilmington. When I was on school vacation in Salisbury, I learned more about life and living. I remember PaPa used to say he got his "Edg e ka shun from the school of hard knocks." Well I learned a lot from under MaMa's kitchen table. She and her lady friends used to get together once a week and work on piecing their quilts together. They would sit around her table sewing and gossiping about everyone and everything. I usually played with my Shirley Temple doll which Mom had finally given back to me. I was very quiet because I didn't want to miss a thing. I heard the most amazing stuff. I didn't understand a lot of what they were talking about. I wondered why they talked about how disgusting it was for Miss Brown to entertain so many truck drivers. They often called her "an old hoe." Why would they call a nice lady like Miss Brown an old hoe? They also thought it was terrible her daughter, poor little Betty Sue had to have so many uncles. No one could have too many uncles! I loved all my mother's brothers. One time those ladies began discussing the local preacher and lady who sang in the choir. "It's just disgraceful! Besides did you hear about …"

Chapter 59 — Not All Bad

Those conversations were boring to me, so I decided to take a walk with my Shirley Temple nurse doll. I wanted to see if Mom's warning sign was still up on Brown and Naylor Street. It sure was! I laughed out loud.

There was a lumberyard on the left side of the street and a very large building with a chain link fence all around it. The fence was topped with rows of sharp barbed wire. There were some men standing around inside the fence. They were all wearing strange looking clothes, which Uncle Fred had told me were prisoner of war uniforms.

One of the men smiled at me and pointed to my doll. Then he reached into his pocket and took out a small picture of a little girl holding a doll in her arms. He smiled and pointed to the picture. He spoke to me, but I couldn't understand him. He raised both of his hands in the air as if to tell me he had surrendered. Then he pointed to his clothes. Then he smiled and hugged himself and waved goodby. I knew he was trying to tell me he was glad the war was over for him and when the war was really over he would be able to return to his little girl!

My PaPa had always talked to me about the importance of thinking about the choices you make before acting. And my Dad had continued to impress me with the same thing. Even today I can hear them in my mind, *"Right choices can make your life much better in the long run! It's not always wise to take the easy choice which may not reward you with a good result."*

I believed this German was a good man in spite of his wearing this prisoner of war uniform. I think he either had to follow Hitler's orders or get himself and his whole family killed if he chose not to obey his crazy dictator. He felt sure Germany would lose the war. So he made the choice to pretend to obey his evil leader. He had signed up and pretended to be a good German soldier. But he hadn't killed anyone and he managed to stay alive. Now he was a prisoner of war. He was happy and smiling because when it was over he would be going back to his family and his little girl. I knew he had worn the German uniform, but I could see the goodness in his eyes.

This was a neighboring lumberyard that burned in 1929. Unfortunately, the lumberyard mentioned in this 1944 story is dismantled now. Picture courtesy of the Salisbury Fire Department Museum archives

I handed him a candy bar I had in my pocket and ran back to my MaMa.

When I was much older I learned there were a lot of good Germans who risked their own lives by providing safe places for Jews to hide. This led to my believing and understanding all Germans weren't crazy. But the ones who were gave their country a very bad name with the unnecessary atrocities they committed on the Jews and even on some of their own countrymen were definitely insane! So, I finally understood if you give some low class person a lot of control over helpless others he will soon abuse his power to show just how important he thinks he is! I prayed silently, "*God protect us from such people!*"

Chapter 60 — Come Home

Mom, at home in Wilmington, got another frantic telephone call from Aunt Edna. She said their father had been getting dizzy spells and staggering around a lot. She had the new doctor in Salisbury come to his house and examine him. Doctor Madison told Aunt Edna her father had a warning heart attack. He gave him some pills and said, "Lee, you are going to have to stop working so hard and you cannot live alone out here in the country all by yourself now." Aunt Edna tried to talk her Pa into staying in Salisbury with her. His answer had been an emphatic "No!". He wouldn't mind a short visit for a day but he had no intention of moving into her house. He said she had enough to put up with her Ma, and her daughter Nina and her two kids. "Besides," he said "you ain't even got a bed where I can sleep." Aunt Edna had moved from Short Street into a larger house on North Division Street. But she still had only two bedrooms. She was taking care of her grandchildren, Joann and Bobby, while her daughter, Nina, was at work. The three of them slept in one of the bedrooms. MaMa slept in the other one and I slept with her when I went for a visit. Aunt Edna slept on the sofa in the living room. He also knew she had to go to work at seven in the morning at the Jackson Shirt Factory around the corner. He argued after MaMa left him and moved to Aunt Edna's he had stayed by himself for the last five years. He said he was making out quite well and was "set in his ways". "Besides,"

Lee Bahnum Ruark

he continued on, "I've got my animals to feed. Who is going to look out for them?" Aunt Edna was really worried. Major, Sully, and Blue had all died a year ago. But he didn't seem to remember. He was getting awfully absent-minded lately.

Aunt Edna pleaded, "Janey please come home! We really need you!"

Mom quickly talked this over with Dad and called Aunt Edna right back. She told her we were leaving for the Shore immediately and asked her to stay with their Pa until we got there. She and I left right away and she drove very fast. We were in Salisbury before nightfall. I held on tight and prayed with my eyes closed all the way. It was a blessing we didn't get killed or stopped by the police for speeding. Mom still had no driver's license!

Chapter 61 — Strange Behavior

Aunt Edna filled Mom in quietly after PaPa had gone to bed. She told Mom she had stayed last night at PaPa's because she was worried he might fall and hurt himself. During the night she was awakened by the sound of his shot gun. When she dashed into the kitchen she found him mumbling, cussing and arguing, "Drag em! Dam you! Drag em! You ain't going to scare me outta my house!" But there was no one else in the room with him. He told me he had heard someone walking up the steps and letting his suspenders drag on the floor, "Click! Thump, Click, Thump!" Later on, he admitted he didn't see anyone but he was sure it was a ghost who wanted him to leave his house. Mom whispered quietly, "My God, you could have been shot! What did you do?" "To be honest", Aunt Edna replied, "I didn't see a thing but I heard that clicking sound and the air in the room turned frigid." Aunt Edna continued softly, "Pa fell asleep with his gun in his lap and I was afraid to take it away from him. I pulled the quilt laying on the couch around my shoulders and sat very still until the sun came up. He had fallen asleep. When he woke he didn't mention his odd behavior and I didn't either!" Later that day, Mom locked his gun in the trunk of her car.

Chapter 62 — A Schemer and a Dreamer

Mom went to see her brother, Fred, to see if he had any ideas. Get a schemer and a dreamer together and they'll come up with something. Uncle Fred said there was a lot for sale near his house on Ruark Drive. It was large enough to build a good-sized chicken house on. The best news was there was an old schoolhouse in pretty good shape on that same lot. He added it could be easily remodeled into a nice bungalow. And the price was right!

He also said he was doing quite well as a chicken grower for Arthur Perdue. He explained Mr. Perdue had paid all the expenses needed for building his chicken house and putting in the right equipment. It took eight weeks to raise a flock of chickens. When the chickens were sold, Uncle Fred had to pay a specified amount of money to Mr. Perdue from each flock until the chicken house and equipment was paid for. Uncle Fred had to buy the feed from the Perdue feed mills. He also had to pay for the heat and electric required. Uncle Fred laughed, "What is left is all for me!" He convinced Mom it was so easy because everything was automatic. She could have a steady source of income raising the chickens and still be at home to watch over their Pa. He finished up with, "I can come in a jiffy if you ever need me." Now all Mom had to do was convince her Pa she needed him to help and advise her on how to raise chickens.

Everything her brother said made sense and Mom was a good talker. The next morning, she convinced her Pa she and her husband were both sick of big city life and she wanted to move back to Salisbury. Mom told him there was too much evil in Wilmington and she was afraid it would be a bad influence on me.

She told him she was thinking about raising chickens and wanted him to show her how. Mom also told her Pa she was buying the old schoolhouse down from Uncle Fred's place on Ruark Drive. She said she would need him to supervise the remodeling because she didn't know anything about being a carpenter. This wasn't actually the truth, but she wanted her Pa to think he was really needed. He would have seen right through her scheme when he was younger. But he wasn't thinking as clearly now. When she talked about needing him and how they could be partners he bought it all – hook, line and sinker. He was happy about what she was planning. He had always hoped he and Mom could be partners in some kind of business. This could be their chance!

Lee and Janey (Mom) at the farm

Chapter 63 — Dangdest Thing

With her PaPa's supervision and advice Uncle Elmer and Uncle Johnny finally came and built walls so we could have three bedrooms. Uncle Roy found a man claiming to be a plumber. He was hired to install the pipes and fixtures for a kitchen. He told them he could also install an inside bathroom by closing in part of the back porch.

There could have been a big debate here because PaPa had declared loud and clear, "That is the dangdest thing I ever heard of! What kind of a fool would want to put a shit house right inside of their home?" Mom agreed with her Pa so he would feel like he was really in charge. In private she told her brothers she could get an inside bathroom installed later. There was no sense upsetting him. If she did he might not agree to stay with her.

Janey (Mom) picking peaches

Chapter 64 — A Slight Delay

Mom's brothers had planned with her what was needed to change the old schoolhouse into a home for us to live in. Unfortunately, there had been a slight delay in Mom's plans. Her brothers had not completed their remodeling as quickly as they promised. It seemed they had too many other things, like card games and dancing, (or galing) which kept them too busy to actually begin making the changes they had agreed on.

Mom called Dad and told him she had turned her rooming house in Wilmington over to a Real Estate company there. Their agent told her it was a good investment and should sell quickly. It did! She told Dad to stay there in Wilmington until all the settlement papers were signed by the new owners. After that was done, she told him to come down to be with us in Salisbury. With a little encouragement from their Ma and a lot of insistence from Uncle Roy's wife, Aunt Grace, Lee's boys were able to get the old schoolhouse changed into a nice school home. They finished their remodeling within a month.

Chapter 65 – Really Hot

Mom decided she would stay at PaPa's house out in the country because she was afraid for him to be alone. I would have to stay with Uncle Roy and his family in Delmar, Delaware until Mom's brothers finished their alterations. Mom promised Dad it would be just a short time. Uncle Roy's house was kind of like Aunt Edna's house only bigger. He and Aunt Grace had four bedrooms upstairs. There was a big warm stove in the downstairs living room. They also had a large kitchen with inside plumbing. Best of all there was an indoor bathroom.

I had to get dressed in my flannel pajamas in the kitchen where it was warm. Then I ran upstairs and jumped under a lot of quilts on Geneva's bed. The quilts were so heavy I couldn't even turn over. Once I was covered though I was nice and toasty.

Uncle Roy and Aunt Grace had three daughters, Doris Lee, Aleen, and Geneva. Aunt Grace always had a grand manner about her. She gave the impression nothing was ever good enough for her girls and she was determined to raise them to be proper young ladies. Uncle Roy often bragged his wife never lost her temper. She always had a very calm manner about her when she was correcting her girls. They usually remembered the point she wanted to get across to them. One day I heard Doris Lee screaming at her younger sister Geneva, "Get out of my face! I'm so hot I could just knock you down!"

Her mother heard her and called softly from the kitchen, "Doris Lee, honey if you are so hot just go outside and sit there on the step till you cool down." Aunt Grace never yelled like a Ruark. She liked to say, "I'm not a Ruark. I just married one!" Well, sitting on the steps didn't sound like a very serious punishment to me or Doris Lee. She slammed out the door and then realized it was below 32 degrees outside. She didn't even have a jacket. The wind was blowing fiercely, and the steps were covered with ice and snow! She cooled off pretty quickly and Doris Lee never showed her temper after this. No one ever heard her say she was hot again. I always wondered if Aunt Grace's mother made sure she never lost her temper by doing the same thing to her when she was a young child.

Chapter 66 — Burnt Bridges

Mr. Silverman owned all of the Royal Shoe Stores on the east coast. Dad worked for him for ten years. But now Dad told him he had to move to the shore because of family problems there. Mr. Silverman scheduled a meeting with Dad and he said, "Paul, I hate to lose you. You've been an excellent help in our store in Wilmington. I really appreciate you giving me your notice to leave. That will give me time to try and replace you." He handed Dad an envelope and said, "I wrote this letter of reference for your next employer.

They shook hands and Dad said, "Thank you, sir. I've learned a lot from you. It's been a great pleasure working for your company. My wife has sold her boarding house here in Wilmington and is already in Salisbury. I'm supposed to join her there as soon as the settlement papers are all signed by the new owners."

"I do appreciate your character reference. Though I'm not sure I'll be using it right away. I will be working for my wife on their family chicken ranch. Like a woman, she does enjoy being the boss!" They both had a good laugh.

Mr. Silverman spoke again, "My father gave me some good advice when I was a young man like you. He told me, 'Don't burn your bridges behind you. You might need to cross that river again someday'. Now remember you'll always have a job with our company if things don't work out on your chicken ranch."

Chapter 67 — A Good Relatioinship

Mom's brothers had finally turned our old schoolhouse into a rather attractive bungalow. We decided to call it our Schoolhouse Home. We left the school bell on the roof as a reminder of when it had been a school. Mr. Perdue had his men build our chicken house and get it all equipped.

We had our first flock of biddies in. True to his word Uncle Fred came down the drive a lot to advise Mom about raising chickens. I think he enjoyed showing off to his little sister about how smart he was. He didn't have much work to do at his place because Aunt Katherin did all the work necessary to raise their chickens.

Mr. Perdue and Mom had a good working relationship. After a visit to Mom's chicken house, he told his other growers Mom had created a playground for her chickens with music and swings.

She learned chickens are very flighty and if they hear a sudden unexpected noise they will bunch together in a tight corner and the ones on the bottom will smother and die. Mom's answer to that problem was to put a small radio in the center of her chicken house. Her radio played continuous music from the first day until the last day when they were picked up. Her idea was to get them accustomed to noise so they would ignore any sudden traffic sounds. And it worked! Her second problem was the water and feed troughs were balanced on cement blocks. When the chickens drank or ate, they would accidentally turn these blocks over. This caused a wet mess which we had to clean up each day. We also had to reseat the blocks and troughs daily. Mom and I put our heads together and figured out how to solve the problem. First, we got rid of those cement blocks. Then we hung the water and feed troughs by a rope that could easily be raised or lowered to the correct height for the chickens as they grew from biddies to full grown chickens. Now they had their music and their swings, and our work was much easier.

The field manager did not agree on one important point in the contract signed by Mr. Perdue and Mom. He came to inform her they would come pick up her chickens in the morning. Remembering a clause in her contract which said all regular feed would be picked up and a different feed would be fed that last two weeks before they were picked up. The purpose of this clause was to make sure no harmful additives were in the chickens when they were put on the market. Mom reminded him of that clause and he just got into his car and shouted, "See you in the morning" and drove away!

Mom called Mr. Perdue and explained the problem. He told his field-manager, Mom was right and it would only be the normal two week delay.

However, the manager showed up early the next morning with two trucks in mom's driveway. During the night Mom had blocked both driveways. One with her truck and one with her car. Then she got her PaPa's rifle out of the trunk of her car and sat with it on her lap waiting for the field manager to show up in case he had chosen to disregard Mr. Perdue's decision.

Mr. Perdue next arrived on the scene. He ordered the truck drivers to return to the office and told the field manager to meet him at the office. Then he apologized to Mom and said she was right, "a contract was a contract to be kept".

And even today, Mr. Perdue's grandson advertises that Perdue chickens are grown without any additives.

Chapter 68 — All the Comforts

Dad had packed up all of our stuff in Wilmington. The Mayflower Trucking Company moved everything we owned down to our new home in Salisbury. The Greyhound bus brought Dad home to us.

He seemed pleased with our new home. We had a nice living room and three bedrooms. There was a big kitchen with hot and cold running water. We wouldn't need a pump bench or pitcher head pump. There was also a modern propane cooking stove. This meant nobody would have to get up early and light a wood stove to cook on. You just put a quarter in a slot on the top. Then you turned on a knob and it got hot right away. Dad had asked Mom to get us a brand-new refrigerator that didn't need ice to keep our food cold. Dad loved ice cream and he promised to keep our new refrigerator stocked with it for our family. The best part for me was the big shiny woodstove sitting in our living room. Now we could all huddle up around it and stay warm even on the coldest winter nights.

Dad had always been a city boy for as long as he could remember. I wondered what he was going to say when he realized our bathroom was outside and down the path?

Chapter 69 — Smucker's Beware

One memory the Ruarks really enjoyed recalling was the one about Mom's homemade jelly. Most everyone knows the Smucker's Company makes one of the best jellies on the market. I think Mom could have given them some competition though.

It was the month of June and here on the Shore it was the time to pick strawberries. It seemed like they were growing everywhere. Farmers had a bountiful crop and there were signs posted in their fields telling everyone to come and pick as many quart baskets of them as they wanted. It cost just ten cents for a quart basket full of those delicious berries. You couldn't fill the baskets too full because the owners would weigh them. Everyone knew that old saying, 'A quart's a pound the world around!'

Strawberries were always planted in neat rows with no weeds, brambles, or thorns to stick into your fingers. Therefore, children were happy indeed to go picking strawberries! You could just wipe off the little bit of sand on your clothes and eat them right in the field! And that is what the children did. Mom and I ate so many of their berries in the field I'm sure the farmers lost money on us. Mom kept gently reminding me to put some in our bucket. I noticed though she ate quite a few too.

There were a lot of other families in the field and when we children got tired of picking and eating, we'd stop and play some outdoor games or maybe even take a nap under a big shade tree. I'm sure some of us dreamed of all the different ways our Moms would fix those berries.

At home we ate our berries in a dish with homemade whipped cream. They were delicious sliced up in our oatmeal or on our pancakes. Mom could make the best strawberry short cake in the world. Sometimes she would mix them in our homemade ice cream. Dad and I got to turn the churner to make this special treat. Even Dad enjoyed homemade ice cream better than the store-bought kind. Those were some of the good old days which some people remember and still talk about today.

We had picked so many berries this time Mom decided to make some strawberry jelly we could enjoy in the cold wintery days of the coming December. She let me help her wash, cap, and slice them up. Then she got down her old spaghetti pot she used for nearly everything she cooked. She put in a layer of strawberries and put a layer of sugar on top. She continued until it was almost full. Then she filled it slowly with water until it was nearly to the top. Finally, she put the large lid on the top of her pot. She then set it on the shelf in the kitchen pantry. She explained the sugar would soak through the berries and make them even sweeter. Then she planned to cook it very slowly and can it in quart-sized Mason jars which were used for preserving foods. She and MaMa said it was too expensive to buy our fruits and vegetables from the store in those metal cans.

Both MaMa and PaPa always complained and said metal cans gave a bad taste to the food so we used our glass Mason jars. They let me help by washing out the jars because I had such little hands. I never grumbled or thought this chore of washing jars was actually work. It was just fun! I was as proud as the day MaMa let me clean those fish a long time ago. We did a lot of canning whenever it was the season for different foods which grew in our gardens. Sometimes we'd trade for something different with our family or neighbors.

Chapter 70 — Oh Excuse Me

MaMa and PaPa often said they couldn't understand why folks up in the city were jumping out of those tall buildings during the Great Depression. PaPa explained, "It was most likely because folks had lost their jobs and didn't have no money saved to buy food. MaMa would usually say, "It's likely they were like the lazy grasshopper and the hard-working ants." Then she would tell the story for the zillionth time. But we did like her telling it.

Oh, excuse me. I have wandered away from Mom's pot of strawberries sitting on the shelf in the kitchen pantry.

Anyway, Mom got busy with some other project and forgot all about her pot of berries in the pantry. Unfortunately, she also caught a bad cold and had to stay in bed for two weeks. When she was able to get out of bed, she remembered her pot of strawberries. She brought it out and set it on the kitchen cupboard. She tasted it cautiously with a spoon.

PaPa came in and said, "Lord All Mighty, Janey! Ain't they the pot of berries you fixed three or four weeks ago? There ain't nuthing you can do now except just throw them out!"

Mom took another taste and mumbled, "Not too bad." She was the thrifty one in the Ruark family.

Violetta and Sarah Martha (MaMa) picking blackberries

She wasn't about to throw them out. She remembered the stories of the great Depression and the war and how food had got to be so scarce.

She well understood the old saying, "Waste not. Want not!" She did not want to waste all those berries and all of her sugar. No Siree! She just added some fresh water and a little more sugar. She put the lid on her pot and cooked them very slowly. She reasoned the heat would kill any germs in her berries. When she thought they were done she took another little sip. "Mmm Not bad! Not bad at all!" After sealing them tight in our quart Mason jars she put them carefully back on the pantry shelves to wait for the cold dreary winter time.

Chapter 71 — Mom's Happy Jelly

It was now Christmas and Mom had learned a long time ago the best gift to give someone for Christmas was something you had made. So, she carried a couple of jars of her strawberry jelly over to Uncle Fred and Aunt Katherin.

Around the middle of February Aunt Katherin asked Mom if she could spare a couple more jars of her strawberry jelly. Mom said happily, "Of course, I'm glad you enjoyed it so much. I wasn't sure if you would like it."

Aunt Katherin laughed, "It wasn't me who enjoyed it! It was Fred! One day he got up so grumpy I thought I had married a bear. He humphed and growled so much and kept finding fault with everything. He just kept looking for an argument. I thought he might be hungry, so I fixed him a couple of your strawberry jelly sandwiches and a cup of coffee. His personality changed almost immediately! It was like a miracle cure! I couldn't figure out why. But I hoped it was the jelly. From then on, every time he'd get grouchy I'd fix him a couple of your jelly sandwiches and a cup of coffee. He'd sweeten right up!" PaPa had been listening to their conversation. He burst out laughing, "Janey, is Katherin talking about the berries I told you to throw out? You foolish gal! Your jelly has fermented into a good wine! If you ever decide to sell any of it you'd best put a fancy label on it saying, Janey's Happy Jelly!"

Well Mom never got into the jelly business. When her jelly was gone she never made any more. So Smuckers remained the king of good jelly. But we had a lot of laughs about Mom's Happy Jelly!

Chapter 72 — Too Hard

Again, MaMa showed up on our front porch just for a visit. Aunt Edna had told her my Mom and Dad were having a hard time trying to tend to their chickens and taking care of PaPa too.

"Oh, Ma I just can't do it all by myself twenty-four seven! I don't know what to do! If I leave Pa alone to check the chickens he takes off like a shot. As you know we live here right close to the main highway. Yesterday I had to hunt him down and I caught him heading for Delmar just like a rambling rose! When I asked him where he was going he said he just wanted to stretch his legs a bit! Paul is a better shoe salesman than he is a chicken farmer, but he really does try to help. I just don't know what I can do!"

"Honey, your Ma is here now to help you. That's why I've come here for a visit!" "Oh Ma," Mom wailed," I can't burden you with my problems!"

"Baby, you ain't no burden to me. We are family and I thought you knew that's what families do! We always help one another!"

Lee Bahnum (PaPa) and Janey (Mom) at her "Chicken Ranch"

Chapter 73 – Gentleman of Leisure

Mom was trying to take care of PaPa and help Dad raise chickens. My job was to go to school and keep my grades up. MaMa was a great help even though PaPa would often argue and say, "I don't need no babysitter. I'm old enough to take care of myself!"

He seemed to be a strong man with good health for his age. None of us had seen any staggering or dizziness lately.

He blamed his tiredness on the fact he wasn't doing any good healthy work as he was used to. To cover up the fact his strength was failing he would brag that now he was a gentleman of leisure.

To avoid boredom, PaPa had even helped us make a root cellar where we could keep things like apples, oranges, cabbage, and both Irish and sweet potatoes over the winter for a very long time. Those vegetables and one of our chickens always made a good meal.

Lee (PaPa) and Violetta and their own chickens

Chapter 74 — Possible

PaPa needed to get his medicine prescription refilled because he was almost out of his heart pills. So Mom insisted on taking him in to see the doctor, who wanted him to go to the hospital for a checkup. In spite of all his fussing and arguing Mom won and took him to the hospital. "That's what I get for having a hard-headed girl like Janey! She gets the best of me every time we have a disagreement," he fussed. His voice had a touch of pride in the fact she was able to get the best of him. No one else ever had. Of course, he didn't see any real need to go to the hospital. He said, "I gave in just because I wanted her to shut the hell up!"

In the hospital it took the nurse and a strong attendant to finally get him into bed. Mom and I waited down the hall until we thought he had settled in. Then we started walking toward his room. We were only halfway there when we heard his loud booming voice. It was not a happy sound, "No you ain't!"

The nurse spoke in a gentle but persistent tone, "Now Mr. Ruark I'm a nurse and your doctor said I had to bathe you."

"I don't care what you are nurse or doctor! Dag Nab It! You are still a woman and you ain't giving me no damn bath!"

We didn't know how long this conversation had been going on. But they were both locked toe to toe like two stubborn goats and neither one of them was going to give an inch. We stood outside the door to his room watching, listening, and waiting to see which one would eventually give in.

They continued their verbal battle. Mom and I were having a hard time choking back our laughter.

"Please Mr. Ruark let's just try to get this done as soon as possible." There was a long silence.

Then we heard his familiar laugh. He shouted gleefully, "That's the answer! You can wash me down as far as possible. And you can wash me up as far as possible and I'll just wash possible myself!"

Mom grabbed my hand and we walked quickly back to the hospital entrance.

We stood outside and had a great laugh. After giving them time enough to do all their washing we went back inside and had a nice visit with my PaPa, the sweetest but most stubborn man in the whole world.

After their tests the doctor said PaPa still had a serious problem with his heart and should just take it easy for a while. Then the doctor wrote him a prescription for some more heart pills and sent him home with us.

Lee (PaPa) and his ever-present hat

Chapter 75 — No Fool

MaMa pulled me onto her lap and said, "Land Ah Goshen child, I can't believe how tall you are! Your legs are almost as long as mine. I ain't got me no baby no more. You are getting to be a grown up young lady. But I can still tell you to cut your own switch and I can still give you a good switchin' with it. So you'd best behave yourself!"

After getting her suitcase unpacked MaMa took charge. She cooked and cleaned for PaPa stayed with us as long as he needed her. She made sure he got his medicine on time and fixed him tasty meals. He had always loved her cooking and had a hearty appetite. As she said, she was "no fool!" She didn't try and force him to do anything. She just kind of coaxed and teased him into doing what he needed to do.

Sarah Martha (MaMa) and Lee Bahnum (PaPa) Ruark

Chapter 76 — It Takes a Sneak

PaPa grumbled almost all the way home from the hospital. "Danged pills don't do no good anyway. These doctors today are nothing like good old Doc Wilson. He was the only good one I ever knew. Today doctors just want to take most all your money as long as you take their danged pills. When you die the undertaker gets the rest of it! At a funeral I ain't never seen a car following the dead man's hearse with any money he thought he was going to keep!"

One day shortly after the visit to the doctor Mom was washing clothes. She checked PaPa's pants pockets before putting them in the washer. She was surprised to find all of the pills he should have been taking were inside his pockets. She was really upset with him and said, "No wonder you're feeling so poorly. Those pills you got from your doctor were supposed to go into your mouth and then into your stomach. They just won't work in your pants pocket!"

PaPa was embarrassed to be caught but he covered it up by laughing loudly and saying, "That's my little smarty pants, Janey! You can't pull the wool over her eyes! Yes sir, she's just like my aunt Lady Jane from my old country!"

PaPa had been an ace putting his pills between his teeth and the inside of his mouth. When I tried to get him to take his medicine or eat something or do anything he'd either say "No period" or he'd just pretend to comply. I certainly had been no match for him. Mom realized he could not be trusted to take any medicine, but she had to tend to the chickens.

My no-nonsense MaMa took charge again. "Janey you just go on and do what it is you have to do with a clear head. The ole fox! If he fooled me once then shame on him! But if he fools me twice shame on me! I trusted him to be swallering his pills, but I'm done with trusting him now. Don't you worry none neither. We were together long enough for me to learn his little sneaky ways. I promise you he will get all of his medicine and eat more regular from now on. She confided in me later she would just mash up his pills and tuck them into his applesauce which he dearly loved. Every once in a while, she'd laugh, wink at me, and say, "It takes a sneak." I knew she meant it takes a sneak to catch a sneak.

Chapter 77 — Two Peas in a Pod

PaPa seemed to be getting stronger. Our fear of another heart attack was beginning to fade. He was beginning to act more like his mischievous old self again. I remember Mom asking him to give me a talking to about dating and dressing in a proper manner. She was really worried about the way kids were behaving these days. She said they had no respect for their elders. Girls were too familiar with the boys and everyone dressed in a very sloppy way. PaPa told me they had it a lot better in his day. When he picked up his gal it was in a horse and buggy. His eyes just sparkled when he told me he didn't have to worry about traffic or steering a car down a busy street. He'd just throw the reins over Major's neck and leave the driving to him. Then he could concentrate more on his spooning. "Well, that's what they called it in those days." Mom was just seething. The redder she got the more colorful he'd paint his picture of courting. He did agree with her concern about being more modest and dressing properly until you were married. He said, "Young folks don't keep anything for a surprise these days. It was a lot more exciting when a young feller had to bend down and act like he was tying his brogans just to get a glimpse of a young lady's ankle as she climbed up into a wagon or surrey. It's good to keep a young feller interested because then he will always come back and try again!"

Mom quickly interrupted and said, "Thank you Pa. You've been a big help. Come on now Violetta, I need you to help me with the dishes." PaPa laughed his wicked little laugh and said, "Aw Janey you know Sarah has done all the dishes. I want to tell Violetta about the courting in a bundling bed." Mom just about shrieked, "Come on Violetta! We'll get Pa some ice cream and some for you too." Dad came into the room just then. He sat down beside PaPa and said, "Bring me some too hon. I want to hear about this bundling bed. It might be real interesting." Mom kind of smiled and said, "You two men are so much alike! What one can't think of the other one does. You're like two peas in a pod!" Then PaPa and Dad shared a hearty laugh together.

PaPa and Dad were great conspirators. They always loved to tease Mom together and get the best of her. She usually took it in a good-natured way and we had a lot of laughs and happy times to remember and treasure.

Chapter 78 — Clogging and Grinning

MaMa had been a tremendous help with PaPa. Once again, we were snug as bugs in a rug. Everything was going along pretty smoothly. Aunt Edna's boy, Norman, was very fond of PaPa and used to visit him often. One night, Norman told him there was no place for his friends to just hang out and he wished they could come and visit with him. PaPa loved company and he missed having his old drinking buddies around. Norman was surprised and pleased when he said excitedly, "Well you could ask them to come on out with you next time you come for a visit. It'll be nice to have some noise in this old place again! It's been too quiet in here for too long!" The next day Norman asked Mom and Dad if they thought it would be alright. They both thought it was a great idea. And Norman's friends were happy to go with him to visit his grandfather. PaPa would entertain them with stories about when he was a young boy. He could really get them laughing when he told about his courting days or some of the pranks his young boys had got into. He would even bring his fiddle out and play it for them. They loved hearing him sing, "The Wahbash Cannon Ball" and would join him in singing the chorus. Even now, so many years later, if it is very quiet and I listen real intently I can still hear them singing.

> "I hear that train ah coming.
> It's coming down the track.
> I'm going to leave this ole town
> and I ain't never coming back!
> Listen to the rattle, the rumble, and the roar.
> It's the Wahbash Cannon ball!"

Then he would do the most amazing thing with his old

fiddle. I swear he could make it sound just like a train going down the track and blowing its' shrill whistle! "Chug Chug Chug Chug! Whooo Weee!". PaPa even showed his new friends how to do some old-fashioned clogging and in their excitement, they would often jump up and start dancing. Our living room was filled with excited laughter and happy sounds. PaPa would just keep on playing, singing, clogging, and grinning. Like MaMa used to say, "He looked just like an ole possum chewing on a yeller jacket!" Everyone had a great time especially PaPa. He was a very congenial host and seemed to enjoy having Norman's friends around. But promptly at nine o'clock he'd give his little cough, lean down, untie his brogans and set them under his chair. Then he'd give a little laugh and say, "Well, folks it's gettin past my bedtime so I'll just be tuckin it in. Now, you all just make yourselves to home and help yourself to the food and sodas."

Mom and MaMa had always made sure there was more than enough snack foods and sodas in the refrigerator for everyone.

Chapter 79 – Remembering

Mom had bought a rocker for her Ma just like the one she had bought for her Pa. They both sat out in the front yard in their rocking chairs with me and they did a lot of talking about the old days. Sometimes they'd just sit real silent and think about their life together. Other times you might hear them burst out with a lot of loud laughing at some happy memory they had shared.

One day he and MaMa were sitting in their rockers in the front yard. I was sitting on the steps listening to their talking because I was still collecting memories for our Ruark quilt.

Sarah Martha (MaMa) and Lee Bahnum (PaPa)
remembering

PaPa asked MaMa, "Do you remember the neighbor who wanted to name her newborn son in honor of Ulysses S. Grant? The midwife who filled out the birth certificate wasn't a very good speller and wrote his name as Useless. MaMa laughed loudly and added, "Yes, I do! He tried hard to live up to that name. I never saw him do nothing except sit on his porch and wave when someone walked by."

MaMa continued, "That reminds me of Harvey Hastings! Remember he had the habit of always being late for any occasion and saying,' Better late than never!'" PaPa slapped his knee laughed even louder than before! "Yep, people wondered why he couldn't keep a job for long. I reckon his bosses got tired of him showing up late so often at work and saying, 'Better late than never!' "

Chapter 80 — Get My Hat

Many pleasant evenings were spent with us all gathered around our old wood stove. Those good times passed too quickly as we began to notice PaPa's memory was getting worse. He had started mumbling to himself just a bit lately.

One day he and MaMa were sitting in their rockers in the front yard. I was sitting on the steps listening to them talking. I wanted to remember their tales and tell them to my own children someday. MaMa and I heard PaPa mumble, "I reckon I'm just about ready now. It's about time to get this over with. Lord willing and the creek don't rise I'll see our darling son Afrey who left us too soon. I see him now! There he is! Wait Afrey!" He paused briefly. Then he spoke louder and more clearly, "Sarah, get my hat." Thinking he probably wanted to take a little stroll to visit Uncle Fred, she went inside and brought his ever present straw hat out to him. He placed it on his head, took his cane in hand and stood upright. Then with a broad smile and a gentle sigh he sat back down for the last time. Lee Bahnum Ruark was gone now but he continues to live on in the telling and retelling of the stories of his life, never to be forgotten by his family and those lucky enough to have known him.

Even with the passing of PaPa, *there's still more to the Ruark Quilt...*

Lee Bahnum ready to go

Author's Bio

Violetta Elrod wrote the *My Family Quilt* book series as an encouragement to future generations. The first book, *My Family Quilt*, tells of her grandparent's life on the Eastern Shore in the early 1900s. This second book, *A Woman Scorned*, is the true story of her mother, Virginia, who in the 1930s and 1940s, demonstrated that same spirit needed to succeed. She wanted to record the true struggles and successes of these pioneers, who like Sarah Martha and Virginia helped build this country over a century ago. To remind the young people of today that as Lee Bahnum used it say, "it ain't over as long as you're above ground."

www.ingramcontent.com/pod-product-compliance
Lightning Source LLC
Chambersburg PA
CBHW080403170426
43193CB00016B/2794